MW00711218

Homeland Security
The Impact of Human Decisions

Closing the gap between strategy and implementation

Jephtah Lorch

Homeland Security: The impact of human decisions

Copyright © 2017 Jephtah Lorch

ISBN-13: 978-965-7569-04-7

Contents

The blind visibility we plan for
is what we wish will be sure to happen within reality's
uncertainty.

Dedicated to the front-line security agents,
Your hard work and dedication are truly appreciated.

Introduction

I am sitting in one of America's international airports, a gateway to the world, contemplating my recent security experience. As always, this is a crowded environment, and the TSA agent forgets to strip me of my belt, making me wonder why I took off my shoes. We feed the X-ray machine with our belongings and queue in front of the full-body X-ray scanner awaiting our moment of truth. It is slow, very slow, and the queue becomes longer and longer. TSA agents are running around trying to understand what the problem is (the slow machine combined with an operator who, rightly so, wouldn't miss an ant). With the queue building up, someone orders the opening of another scanner, only this time it's a metal-detecting gate, and the passenger flow resumes. Still standing in line, I was trying to understand what exactly the TSA was looking for. Metals detected by the metal detector or hard objects identified by the X-ray machine?

Being in the X-ray line, I was stuck, but the queue suddenly resumed its movement when a TSA agent announced: "Men only!" *So much for women's lib*, I thought while moving into the full-body scanner and standing with my hands up. "Stand here," I was instructed as the X-ray machine identified my plastic reading glasses and an item I never had, but the agent was forced to look for because the machine erroneously found it. Passenger flow through the metal detector was seamless, fast, and without any gender issues–or alarms, for that matter. So, the means became the goal: clear every passenger using any screening method, even if those methods identified different types of objects.

The huge HLS machine, employing hundreds of thousands of agents in the US, is fulfilling a mission. The question raised herein is whether it is fulfilling its mission the *right way* to achieve its goals. To give one example, in 2015, the TSA failed 67 out of 70, or 95%, of arms and explosives smuggling tests run by agents of the Department of Transportation.

Homeland Security is meant to protect citizens against criminal, terror, and other attacks whose profile and risk are defined from time to time by HLS leadership. Possible attack scenarios are analyzed and defined, but for some reason, attacks aren't really prevented, because locations shift, and targets and methods change.

What is impeding us from stopping these attacks? Advance identification of perpetrators? Attack potential? Are the attacks happening in less protected sites? Does the problem lie with the perpetrators and their methods, or with us, the secu-

2

rity people? Is it their imagination and determination, or the thinking and methods used by security and law-enforcement policymakers and instilled in their organizations?

9/11 was a turning point in domestic security for developed countries: hatred was brought to America, and the infamous attack signaled the rise of terror in Europe. Terror ceased being "noise" or "nuisance"; it became a real risk, a mission, an idea, a multi-headed Cyclops, an extension of crime and cooperator thereof. But there are differences: crime needs low profile, terror seeks high profile. Government in turn seeks structure and predictability, while terrorists and criminals are cunning and agile, delivering their lethal mosquito sting.

Thus, being deep inside the Third World War, which is driven by religious preachers and power seekers, the question is: Is the West ready to confront those waging war on our way of life? Is the West ready to clearheadedly and decisively meet the adversary, not on his terms but on ours?

The answer seems to be a halfhearted yes. Massive organizations are limited by policymakers and decision makers who, for the sake of political correctness, refuse to acknowledge the source of World War III–an ideological and religious war justified by many through the Qur'an. Nor, in many cases, are these organizations free to fight crime the way crime works against society.

This book discusses the oxymoron of Homeland Security in its wider sense, trying to understand if what is being done and the way it is being implemented can really meet the next terror or mass-crime attempt. My conclusion is "not really": the first line of defense is clearly a follower of attacks, and sometimes a weak responder that needs to be improved and strengthened. This book seeks to create and increase awareness to alternative thought patterns, to refresh perspectives and bring new life into the planning, adaptation, and response of security organizations. The goal is to leverage what exists, but also enhance its flexibility, its human flexibility: personal, mental, and under duress. It is about connecting theory and practice and understanding the realities of constant change.

Oscar Wilde said: "We teach people how to remember; we never teach them how to grow." I believe it's time to grow.

Let us have a deeper look at who our perpetrators are, two central groups: terrorists and criminals. Today's terror–and let us be explicit about it–is Islamic driven. Islam is the second biggest religion in the world with approximately 23% of the world's population (2010). Of these, some 40% are considered Arab Muslims like those living in the Gulf states, Iraq, Syria, Egypt, Libya and other Middle Eastern and North African countries. For reasons not discussed in this book, it is in and from Arab Muslim cultures that today's world terror has grown, reaching monstrous dimensions costing some countries their existence, and millions their lives and homes. Some of this happens because of Western leadership's mistaken understanding of Muslim and Arab culture. To clarify, the fact that militant groups wage war in the name of Islam does not mean all Muslims are terrorists. This book does not imply, ex-

4

plicitly or implicitly, that all Muslims are terrorists; it reflects on the fact that most if not all of today's worldwide terror is done in the name of Islam and is exacerbated by cultural misunderstandings.

The result is chaos in Syria, Libya, Iraq, North Nigeria, Turkey, Afghanistan, and other countries in which Islamic groups seek to create havoc on their way to an Islamic Caliphate with far too many self-proclaimed leaders. Many Western leaders fail to understand the drivers and cultures of these violent and destructive forces, so much so that Western countries indiscriminately open their borders to absorb refugees at the risk of the country's own security and sometimes culture, as seen in Belgium, France, the UK, Germany, and, to a much lesser extent, in the US as well.[1]

While terror seeks and thrives on chaos, organized crime, as violent and cruel as it can be, needs economic and social stability to thrive; it seeks to form a part of culture, not overtake it. It embraces social and economic stability, which is the growing and feeding bed of criminal economy. It can also be argued that the criminal death toll is much higher than the death toll terrorism inflicts in the western world yet, crime does not seek to change western culture and values while terror does.

Despite the differing strategies, organized crime and terror share tactics. Both need smuggling routes, money-laundering

---

[1] See February 1993 bombing of the Twin Towers http://edition.cnn.com/2013/11/05/us/1993-world-trade-center-bombing-fast-facts/

opportunities, stealth operations, and sources of income. ISIS[2] in Iraq, Al-Qaeda in Afghanistan, Hezbollah in Lebanon, and Boko Haram in Nigeria all have drug-smuggling and money-laundering networks to finance their operations. When lacking, for example, retail networks for drugs, terror organizations cooperate with criminals in different countries. In their attempt to expand, they also establish dormant operations in many countries just like Iran did in Argentina when, in 1992, it bombed the Israeli Embassy killing 29 people, and in 1994 when it blew up the Jewish Cultural Center in Buenos Aires, killing 85 people. This pattern continues into Europe: the 2006 uncovered plot to blow up several planes flying from London to the US[3]; the 2015 Paris attacks on Charlie Hebdo and Hypercacher killing 12. In Asia, we should remember the 2002 attack in Bali leaving 202 dead, mostly Australians and Britons.[4]

Why is the West allowing criminal and religious chaos to draw it into constant drug battles, money-laundering chases, and religious wars? What is the oxymoron paralyzing the West? It is a cultural gap, a deep misunderstanding of adversaries, their motives, their culture, and even their determination? This understanding must reach all the way to Homeland Security field agents, so they can better perform their preventive duties.

This book is about people, the human spirit, and protecting

---

[2] Also, known as ISIL, DAESH, IS.

[3] https://www.theguardian.com/uk/2009/sep/07/plane-bomb-plot-trial-verdicts

[4] http://www.bbc.com/news/world-asia-19881138

freedom. It is about life realities of good, dedicated security people and their daily challenges, presented from different angles.

HLS: What It Is and What Makes It Unique

War is like business: there are never two alike.

First responders operate from emergency to emergency and live from event to event. Their nature is reactive and, in many cases, preventive. Yet, in some respects security forces are different, they also drive (other) first responders because their main role begins with detection and prevention of malicious activities, not only with *post-event* reaction. The need for post-event response of security forces arises from the inability to detect and prevent all malicious activities to begin with. There are cases in which the failure to detect and prevent malicious activities is unjustified, when for example, intelligence was available, but for some reason got "lost in the system", while in other cases the failure to prevent may have been more acceptable because of the very local nature of an event like "Lone Wolf" attacks.

Security organizations seek to identify knowledgeable and connected intelligence sources whose information is used to capture criminal and terror rings. The success of a security organization is reflected by its ability to detect and prevent potential malicious events as early as possible; avoid them altogether; or, if challenging, contain events and minimize the number of victims and damage. The nature of security also needs supporting forces like local police, Red Cross, fire departments, and hazmat, which affect the readiness and efficacy of other first responders.

When we speak of security organizations, we're talking about a variety of bodies covering different disciplines and responsibilities. In the United States, these bodies include the CIA (covering international activities), the FBI (covering national activities), the DEA (focusing on drug trafficking), the TSA (transportation security), ICE (covering immigrations and customs), NSA (covering signal intelligence), and all the way to state and local police forces.

The biggest challenge for these agencies is identifying the rotten apple in the barrel, separating the perpetrator from the innocent crowd. An additional challenge is sharing information, seeing the "same picture," and offering a reasonably unified response to developing and rolling threats.

These perpetrators have many facets, with different risks associated with each. Terrorism, for example, is about loss of lives, assets, cyber security, and knowledge, and/or infrastructure damage aimed at causing havoc and reducing citizens' trust in their government and their way of life. Organized and drug related crime are about the "big money" by creating an ongoing negative impact on communities and on social and public order.

Whom Are We Protecting Against?

The role of security organizations is to protect our way of life, our values, culture, economy, and safety–all that makes Western countries what they are. Part of what Western democracies offer is liberalism, openness, opportunity, creativity, predictability, safety, and the acknowledgement of their global social responsibility to weaker countries. It is this predictability and safety that attracts immigrants. A macro view dictates that this openness remains, irrespective of whether you are Republican or Democrat, Green or Social Democrat. The US thrives because of immigration. But this openness also allows easy entrance and assimilation of perpetrators; the exploitation of freedom used to commit malicious acts.

For these and other reasons, democracies are the perfect target for terrorists, drug lords, smugglers of all types, and fugitives. No more bank or train robberies–today it is about exploiting the same technologies and routines that serve our lifestyle. The rewards, whether financial or ideological, are big: an open, liberal society is easier to infiltrate than a dictatorship; and justice, if necessary, is likely to be laxer than that found in totalitarian regimes.

However, today's terrorism is led by a cultural war between Western values and certain, specific Middle Eastern doctrines. Terrorism is a tool in a war designed to destroy Western culture. It exploits what we consider the strengths of democracy to create deadly havoc, thereby converting those democratic strengths to weaknesses. Not only terrorists, but also criminals like drug lords and smugglers, exploit the same openness to enrich and empower themselves. They exploit it because Western democracies are the lowest-hanging fruit: rich, accessible, and forgiving–unlike, for example, closely knit tribal cultures.

All these perpetrators share a similar cunning along with similar methods: smuggling paths, banking routes, communication methods, pre-operation preparation, and intelligence-collection methods. Close analysis of these and other activities can help us define and identify who exactly we're up against. Some of these similarities include:

- Vicious and self-centered goals, often at the expense of the well-being of others;

- Relatively small, well-organized, and mostly flat hierarchies;

- Creative, fast-moving, and stealthy tactics, allowing for long preparation times before surprise attacks;

- The enforcement of their power with violence and money;

- Harsh, uncompromising codes of conduct based on fear, leading to nearly zero defection;

- A single person or small group usually serving as judge, prosecutor, and hangman, with no appeals and certainly no human rights. Orders are to be obeyed, not questioned;

- Common access routes, legal and illegal, and collaboration in many activities. Criminals allow terrorists the use of their smuggling routes, for example, in return for the terrorists' protection of those routes, or for arms or other give-and-take arrangements.

It is important to remember, though, that while many perpetrators share thinking and operating modes, their "language" is different because their wares and goals differ.

Whose Human Rights? The Perpetrators' or Mine?

Security organizations, more specifically HLS, in developed and democratic countries, which are those in need of the most protective security) are devised considering human and civil rights, privacy, and other aspects in line with personal freedom. This is the openness and liberalism that we consider the strengths of democracy. However, in many cases, more intrusive physical and personal searching that violates Western civil-rights ideals is required.

This dichotomy, between what we believe is "right" or "humane" and what is necessary to prevent perpetrators from committing crimes, is what both terrorists and criminals exploit. But when it comes to civil rights, the real question is whose do I protect first? Do I relax the public's rights to save them from a terror attack? Or, do I respect the public's rights, thus lowering the probability of preventing such an attack? Do I apply my values to perpetrators who do not respect my values, or do I protect my home and values while selectively denying the rights of freedom to certain high-risk persons? And yes, there is a risk that in the process innocent people will be hurt, but innocent people will be hurt if malicious activities are not prevented. Thus, the question is *when* will innocent people be hurt, not *if*.

The balance between citizens' civil rights and perpetrators' is very delicate; it involves humans whose decisions are sometimes emotional, biased, or otherwise not objective. Yet, decisions need to be made. Sometimes the few are deprived to save the whole, especially when terror is concerned.

The June 12, 2016 mass-shooting terrorist attack in a gay nightclub in Orlando, Florida left 49 victims dead and at least 53 wounded. The assailant, Omar Mateen (29) is a US-born citizen of Afghan decent. He was questioned several times by the FBI, but no hard evidence justifying legal action was found. The November 13, 2015 attack in Paris, centering around the Bataclan theater, was committed by Belgian-born citizens led by a Syrian refugee,[5] much like the case with the 2016 Brussels Airport bombing and the axe attacks in Wurzburg and Dusseldorf in Germany. The San Bernardino attack was prepared and

---

[5] http://www.telegraph.co.uk/news/worldnews/europe/france/12000822/
Paris-attacks-policeman-gives-first-account-of-Dantes-Inferno-scene-at-Bataclan-concert-hall.html and
http://www.ibtimes.com/amid-bataclan-hostage-crisis-did-paris-police-wait-too-long-rescue-victims-2184336

executed by immigrants who had been welcomed by American laws. As were the 9/11 attacks, early signs of which were misinterpreted or overlooked by a combination of American services. The Fort Hood 2009 shootings were committed by the son of immigrants,[6] and according to reports, there were clear signs of the perpetrator's personal instability that were overlooked by the system but not by peers and superiors. All these cases are events where the civil rights of certain (malicious) individuals were somehow placed above those human rights of society and the public at large. These are high-profile cases, but most others remain unheard of.

"Human rights" is a loaded term, and one that is culturally biased. Take another example, one in which human-rights activists initiated a boycott of a well-known sports equipment manufacturer, claiming that their soccer balls were hand sewn by children in India. Following demonstrations and media exposure, the sports manufacturer caved and saw to it that no children were employed in any of their manufacturing plants. The activists "won," and yet what really happened is that the Indian children simply went to work elsewhere because their families depended on their income. The idea that these children would stop sewing soccer balls and go back to school was impossible for both social and financial reasons. Rich consciences were soothed, "human rights" were dished out, but essentially nothing changed, and the situation of the children may even have worsened since they were laid off and were forced to find fur-

---

[6]   https://en.wikipedia.org/wiki/Nidal_Hasan

ther employment, sometimes far away from their families.

We need to be clear about whose rights we are protecting, and whether we choose to soothe our immediate conscience or protect our way of life, values, and long-term security. Good intentions can be, and sometimes are, misguided. Liberal Europe is currently paying for its short-term emphasis on protecting human rights and openness by experiencing terror attacks. And with every successful attack and subsequent retaliation, terrorists are encouraged and their motivation grows.

Human and civil rights are an important concept, encouraging personal freedoms; and yet we should acknowledge that, like with all generalizations, there are exceptions. It is the job of security organizations and their legal advisors to weigh the issue of rights (both general and specific) against the very freedoms, safety, and security they are to protect. We should not wait for a catastrophe to justify retaliation, which by its nature escalates animosity and death tolls.

What Makes HLS Unique?

Homeland Security is a unique type of organization in both government and corporate worlds. Like other reactive bodies, or first responders like firefighters or the Red Cross, its value is measured through both prevention and event containment. There is no immediate measurable return on investment except that it addresses the social need for security. But that is where the similarities between HLS and other first responders end.

The Red Cross, for example, treats a finite number of medical symptoms and event types, and its medics grow through practice. Firefighters and hazardous-material response teams map risks in their respective areas and ensure that precautions are taken, and that organizations and teams are properly prepared to contain events in their region. In addition, most first responders are on standby awaiting emergency calls.

HLS organizations, on the other hand, operate under a different set of rules.

HLS is first detectors AND first responders. This detection element must be alert 24/7, year-round. This alertness includes staff, equipment, communication lines, chains of command, procedures, and knowledge of strengths and weaknesses. Detection is key to prevention and early action. Thus, there *is* no off time during routine activities.

There are no dispatchers available to brief HLS first responders or to provide additional information. In fact, in many cases the opposite is true: HLS field agents are the first responders and the dispatchers; they are the first who call for backup.

HLS should prevent, not only contain. Unless prior intelligence is available, HLS receives no specific emergency calls, yet it needs to detect and prevent security events. Events occur suddenly, take on- or off-site staff by surprise, and test real-time readiness and response. Detection and prevention of a major security event require imagination, resourcefulness, determination, and ability to react under duress.

The first point, in particular, presents some unique challenges to HLS organizations.

HLS and the Challenges of Pre-Event Detection

Pre-event detection, one of the prime responsibilities of any HLS organization, has an infinite number of threat possibilities created by inventive perpetrators. HLS staff members understand that detecting such risks without prior intelligence is like finding the proverbial needle in a haystack. As a result, preparations and readiness become more complex, including, for example:

- **Prepared** - Security forces must be conceived, recruited, trained, equipped, and ready for malicious scenarios as defined by their leadership, whose responsibility is preparedness. Poor preparation and readiness was evident during the March 22, 2016 terror attacks in Belgium, where intelligence about the terrorists was available but not used. Two of the three coordinated suicide attacks occurred in the Brussels Airport at Zaventem. An hour later, the third explosion struck Maelbeek metro station near the European Union headquarters, leaving 32 dead and over 300 injured. Another bomb was found during a search of the airport. ISIS claimed responsibility for the attacks. The perpetrators belonged to a terrorist cell that had been involved in the November 2015 Paris attacks. The Brussels bombings happened shortly after a series of police raids targeting the terrorist group;

- **Creative** – Alertness of HLS teams should include an element of creativity. Looking only for the last-known threats leaves more opportunities open for perpetrators to succeed with their mission. Take for example the case of Richard Reid, known as the Shoe Bomber, who in 2001 attempted to bring down American Airlines flight 63 from Paris to Miami with explosives hidden in the sole of his shoe. This was a creative attempt to do harm on the part of the perpetrator because shoe-hidden explosives were not considered a threat up until this point. HLS agents were unprepared, leaving Reid free to board the flight despite Reid having been denied flight access the day before. Of course, only in hindsight can we improve our alertness, but if perpetrators are free to come up with creative solutions to execute malicious activities, should not HLS leadership and agents also have that same creativity? However, given the directives, conditions, and pressures agents work under, it is unlikely that their creativity will work as well as the terrorists' creativity;

- **Vigilant** – Security bodies must use constant vigilance, ready to react immediately to suspected and detected threats as well as actual events. Many security organizations are on "relaxed alert" and staffed by otherwise good people who lack fast-response abilities. The 0 to 100% change in pace when a threat materializes confuses many, resulting in poor responses, whether a detection, prevention, or containment response;

- **Attitude** – Because there is often no prior knowledge of a specific risk, security agents must treat all their activities, detection cases, or suspicions as **having high risk potential**. In case of a high-probability or actual event, first responders activate additional response and support groups like physical forces or tactical intelligence;

- **Mechanized** – HLS does depend on technology, but even more so on its staff–the people operating the technology. However, it is impossible to keep humans on tense alert 24/7/365 with consistent use of equipment, detection and response levels;

- **Standardized** – HLS organizations, particularly governmental ones, are massive. Government agencies and bodies employ tens and hundreds of thousands of agents. Maintaining the same performance level throughout the organization given the variety of personalities, work shifts, seasons, education, and threats, is practically impossible. While technical means and operational procedures attempt to standardize detection and responses, they are not always effective or productive because of later discussed limitations of technology.

HLS is certainly a unique body. It combines people and technology and, it is expected to detect, prevent, and react. Over 99% of the time, the body is in a relaxed routine, and yet in a millisecond it may need to flip to active prevention and full-fledged response. All HLS bodies face the unique set of above-mentioned challenges along with their inherent limitations, be these geographic, cultural, or other performance-limiting elements.

Designed and Developed to Meet Specific Threats

Another inherent limitation of HLS organizations is their design: Only a finite set of risks is prioritized and targeted. HLS cannot provide 100% security because it is impossible to target all known (or unknown) potential threats. Therefore, priorities and probabilities are estimated to choose which threats to focus on, especially when considering unknown threats and risks, fantastic as they may be, such as during 9/11.

People, procedures, and systems are then chosen and organized to detect and respond to the threat groups deemed worthy by HLS leadership. Procedures define what agents should look for, how equipment should be used, and how to react in case any threat is detected. And yet in most procedures I have seen, "events and responses" form much of the text and get the most attention and, it is latently assumed that technology will detect the threats such as weapons, liquids, hazardous materials, and data such as facial and fingerprint recognition.

Procedures, as good as they may be, cannot compensate for lack of staff training, nor ensure security in the case of excessive concern for civil rights. Explosive detection, for example, is done randomly rather than based on the profiling of typical perpetrators. This random choice reduces the probability of detection rather than increasing it. It seems that the "system" doesn't trust agents to identify dubious human behavior, odd packages, or suspicious-looking passengers for examination and questioning. Another part of the issue is probably an effort to avoid discrimination and "racial profiling," a problem in line with the above discussion of civil rights. But profilers are used in marketing and advertising and recruiting employees. What is wrong with profiling passengers? Individuals forming the public are as innocent as the typical traveler. This reliance on technology and diminution of the human factor has consequences.

When it comes to technology, detecting a threat is sometimes simply impossible, whether that threat be an explosive charge in someone's underwear or a pistol printed on a 3D printer using non-ferrous materials. Technology does a great job detecting very specific objects or materials, but it lacks flexibility and creativity. Technology will not identify all nervous-looking passengers or other suspicious behaviors, but a well-trained person can.

However, on the human side, as mentioned above, the size and spread of organizations present a limiting factor to HLS, reducing the ability to unify and standardize detection and responses. While technology has the benefit of consistency, humans do not. Despite procedures that seek to educate, train, and standardize the human factor, different personalities, moods, regional cultures, change of work shifts, and even the weather affect repetitive and consistent detection and reaction. To these external factors, we can add staff motivation and personal issues that also affect the quality of human performance, especially when we consider the fact that many security agents choose this career due to lack of alternatives, rather than because they see themselves as career security agents. Thus, there may be an inherent compromise or lack of abilities and motivation to begin with.

The result is that in real life, daily performance of HLS may critically diverge from the vision and threats it is designed to detect and prevent.

Static with Peak Reactions

Another limitation of an HLS body is the above-mentioned challenge of the 0 to 100% change in pace. Detection to reaction, or from routine to emergency response, should be a matter of seconds, but in a massive organization this is difficult. US Navy Seals and other specialized military units are deliberately selected and well trained for such immediate responses, but for practical reasons it is prohibitive to do the same in large civil defense units.

Forcing this large civilian body into immediate action may, furthermore, be risky. Not all agents remember their roles, and under duress may not fully react as expected, and, as a result, may increase their dependency on technology. A variety of small gaps, delays, or local failures then accumulate into a large failure, such as letting a suspect escape, or falling into deceptive traps or distractions. This has often happened in the Middle East when several suicide bombers detonated themselves sequentially. The second bomber awaits the arrival of first responders and curious bystanders and then detonates him- or herself creating further damage and high-impact loss of life.

The change of state from routine to full alert and response in (almost) zero time, puts the entire organization and its co-responders under a great deal of stress, testing their focus, response effectiveness, and coordination. Moreover, in a civilian body far less trained compared to military forces, such an immediate change of state can increase the risk when chaos builds up and the wrong response priority it set, like wrong identification of the perpetrator. However, early intelligence and risk-detection tools increase available response times, allowing HLS bodies to better prepare for a possible event. This brings us to the important role of operational intelligence discussed in a later chapter.

Today's Business of Violence

The sure past is a safe place to dwell on.

Terror as a Business

Terrorism is a business, and a very profitable one, which is why it's become an export product. Modern terrorism developed as a business during the second half of the twentieth century in different parts of the world, including Colombia's FARC, whose leadership never intended to rule Colombia; the new ETA in Spain; the Red Brigades in Germany; FATAH and other Palestinian and Islamic organizations; the famous Ilyich Ramírez Sánchez (alias "Carlos the Jackal"); and ISIS leader Abū Bakr al-Baghdadi.

During the 1960s, socialist, leftist, and separatist terror dominated the scene. Today's terror is mostly Islamic led, expanding rapidly in the Middle East, Central Asia, and Africa. Socialist, leftist, and separatist groups, despite their generally anti-capitalist ideologies, needed money to run their operations and to support their standards of living. Yes, they had dreams, but they never realistically thought they would or could repeat the success of the 1917 Bolshevik revolution that led to the creation of the Soviet Union. These groups ended up becoming basically capitalists, spouting pretexts of freedom, equality or whatever other banner they happened to be flying at the time, that encouraged members to kill and destroy.

Terror was adopted as a tool by many, though its justification drifted. For example, the Palestinian Fatah began its terror activities in the 1950's under a territorial pretext. Nowadays, Palestinian groups like the Iran-backed Hezbollah, Hamas, and the Islamic Jihad practice terror under a religious pretext, exemplifying how a group's "banner" can change over time. Al-Qaeda, ISIS, Jabhat Al Nusra, Boko Haram, and many other similar militant groups continue to fight for a dream they will never achieve, but on the way, they amass fortunes, power, and are controlled by a selected few. I seriously doubt that the dream of an Islamic Caliphate will come true, not only because the democracies that are being fought against are reacting, but also because of power struggles between terror groups and their self-destructive culture that calls for carnage.

On the business and operational side, controlling resources, funds, people, and ideologies within such organizations is difficult, complex, and calls for strict obedience and extreme measures up to killing embezzlers or disloyal members. The above organizations may kill those who wish to leave the way of terror or force them to become suicide bombers to protect their families from death.

The financing of these groups comes from diverse sources,

including donations, state sponsorship, gaining control of oil installations, drugs, contraband, kidnapping, extortion, and looting. While leaders sell ideology, wealth and fear buy them loyalty, weapons, and salaries for their followers. Wealth also reduces patronage competition by establishing the power balance between factions (just like between criminal cartels and gangs). Lebanon's Iran-backed Shiite Hezbollah is slowly learning the limits of its power after losing over a thousand fighters in Syria while protecting President's Assad's regime. Fighter motivation is dropping because they are fighting a war that is perceived as not theirs. Their mission is to conquer Israel, but as their weapons and funding come mostly from Iran who wishes to protect the Assad regime, Iran forces Hezbollah to fight in Syria. Money is also becoming scarce because costs are high: Loss of lives requires that fighters be better paid, and Iran's financial resources dwindled until 2015, when President Obama led the voidance of the sanctions against Iran, refueling their finances.

In addition, many terror groups invest in capitalistic democracies where their wealth grows and is protected. The delay in announcing the death of Yasser Arafat was also related to the control struggle over hundreds of millions of US dollars' worth of financial and other assets that he had under his personal control in Western banks.

The leaders of Palestinian Hamas have a personal net worth[7] estimated (2015) at around 2.6 billion US dollars for

---

[7]   https://www.algemeiner.com/2014/07/28/gazas-millionaires-and-

Khaled Mashal, and a further 2 billion US dollars for Ismail Haniyeh, who resides in Gaza. Their wealth is not the result of meager salaries paid to ideologically driven freedom fighters, nor is it a civil servant's salary. It is loot that comes from places such as UNRWA funding and US and European aid.

These people, and others such as Abu Bakr al-Baghdadi, ISIS's leader and a self-proclaimed Caliph, or Al-Qaeda's Osama Bin Laden, send their people to be killed, yet heavily invest in their personal security. Moreover, while calling on others to become Shahids through fighting Jihad or becoming suicide bombers, they seek to avoid such deaths in their own families. Their death-ridden campaigns then help them conquer not just people but assets, weapons, oil fields, and even power stations, whose output is then sold to local governments. Riches buy power and greedy followers, as in any other business, but then cruelty and terror also buy fearful followers to expand territories.

This fast-growth industry of violence attracts dozens (the US State Department names over forty) of self-proclaimed leaders who use Islamic indoctrination to justify their actions, as seen in Africa, Iraq, Syria, and now, as of 2017, also in Europe. In the US, we see the buds of these organizations emerging, some financed by foreign adversaries.

Their wealth can last if they are on the move, creating havoc, increasing poverty and appeals for Western aid. Apart from its slogans, dreams, banners, and ideologies, this busi-

---

billionaires-how-hamass-leaders-got-rich-quick/

ness of terror does not offer any long-term alternative for its people, food, education, well-being, or future.

Organized Crime and Smugglers

It is perhaps worth taking a moment to compare the business practices of terrorist organizations with other traditionally violent organizations. We can agree that organized crime and smugglers both use violence as a business practice, and yet there are essential differences in motivations and the way violence is employed when compared to terror groups.

Whether discussing organized crime or smuggling groups, they have an interest in a strong economy and public order that help them work in a predictable and financially sound environment. Their use of violence is intended only to exercise power and control within the organization or against targeted victims. Unlike terror, crime seeks low profile by avoiding displays of mass power and generation of chaos. The need for predictability and stability is seen at times when crime groups exercise their power for social purposes as seen in Japan's 2011 Fukushima nuclear disaster, where the Yakuza, a Japanese organized crime syndicate, took part in rescue operations; or São Paulo's *favelas*–low-income urban areas–where order is enforced by criminal gangs.

While chaotic, poor countries grow more crime, but this crime is unable to create great riches unless it infiltrates the government further deepening the people and country poverty.

While I do not wish to minimize the impact that violence of

any kind can have, what is clear is that organized crime groups exploit violence in different ways than terrorist groups. They use violence to grow, manage, and protect their businesses, directing violence mostly (though not always) internally to maintain a predictable, profitable, lower-risk business.

While terror wishes to surprise by using ever-changing patterns, crime seeks stability to build what eventually becomes traceable and identifiable patterns. Thus, the strategies for detection and prevention of criminal and terrorist activities need to be different.

The Challenge of Detection and Prevention

This discussion of violence as a business boils down to one essential question: How do we stop it? Stopping violence is the remit of security organizations. Today's physical organizations–like border, transportation, or industry–all have common characteristics, which mostly reflect their historical development. As is the way with life, these characteristics offer advantages and disadvantages, some of which may become grinding stones as the nature of crime and terror changes. Let's look at some of these characteristics.

The Case of Static and Fixed Solutions

There is no 100% security; we can only strive to improve and reach better and better coverage. When planning security, the question is not only what do I protect, but also what do I sacrifice, what will I not protect, and what is the cost of damage created in such sacrificed zones–be that people, information, or assets.

But security improvement is not all: threats also change in nature–block one path, and perpetrators will find an alternative one. Thus, threat dynamics define changing risks, need for new sensors, budgets, and human profiles, converting these into limiting factors because whatever or whichever solution is put in place today must change with risk and threat scenarios tomorrow.

Let us look at the example of fixed installations. Most installation-related solutions are static or fixed because these installations do not move. Ports, airports, border crossings, military installations, or nuclear power plants, for instance, have perimeters, physical lines that define the proprietary area, and security, all of which are handled in a very traditional manner. There are perhaps guards who patrol, controls at entry points, and control of goods that can or cannot cross the perimeter, in- or outbound. The static nature also reflects security solutions and systems that also tend to be fixed in terms of location and performance-specific equipment, like metal detectors or CCTVs. However, as discussed in the first chapter, adding together the limited capabilities of equipment, which may be perfect at one narrowly defined role but is inflexible and cannot act outside that role, and the potential for inconsistent human performance, leaves gaps identified and exploited by sharp and quick perpetrators.

Another characteristic of fixed security solutions is routine.

Think of guards patrolling set paths at set times and changing shifts at fixed hours. These create employee stability and predictability but also help perpetrator's planning. Such fixed solutions tend to be negatively inflexible, affecting detection and response quality in case of threats and actual events. As much as an organization prepares, plans, and trains, Murphy's Law (*Anything that can go wrong will go wrong*) will catch up and expose our weaknesses. In other words: always expect the unexpected, which is the real essence of security but a total contradiction to the concept and personalities involved in the implementation of such fixed security solutions.

A classic lesson here is that of the famous World War II Maginot defense line the French built to block German attacks from the east. Their doctrine followed the static warfare concept employed during World War I. The Maginot Line failed when the Germans chose to circumvent the fortified line and invade France through Holland and Belgium. The static line was useless against the German maneuver. Looking for backdoors is a tactical warfare tool as old as warfare itself; it was practiced before the Trojan Horse was conceived, in attacking medieval fortresses all the way to modern warfare, and today's cyber-attacks. It was used by the famous Carthaginian commander Hannibal, who between 218 BC and 203 BC crossed the Alps and conquered parts of the Roman empire by following what then was perceived as a most fantastic strategy, just like the 9/11 attacks.

When an attacker is decisive and resourceful, he will suc-

32

ceed in finding and penetrating fixed security locations. As we live in an ever-changing world of threats, falsification, weapon accessibility, 3D printers, chemical weapons, cyber-attacks, and even the changing expectations from and of staff, a new level of awareness and flexibility is required. Increased awareness and knowledge and wider understanding of potential threats and countermeasures is a must. Security should expand well beyond threat types (automatically) defined by the mere choice of equipment we use, by physical characteristics, or standard training. In short, it is more than fixed, static solutions that are required to increase event detection and prevention probability. We need personalities, brains, determination, and flexibility; we need better-trained people and higher trust in them.

Dynamic Security

Dynamic security is the opposite of the static kind; it relies on constant movement, thorough understanding of the threats, lack of routine, and it is based on the dictation of higher-level goals which are then interpreted in the field by the respective commanders. This setup requires better-trained personnel who are "on the prowl" for risks and events. Its advantages include lower capital investments and increased flexibility as compared to static security. The flip side, as stated, is more able, creative, better-trained, and prepared personnel with limited control of the protected area.

The reality is that for best results, both elements—static and dynamic–are combined to follow the chosen security strategy, which is itself derived from understanding of threats, perpetrators, and available defensive resources.

Designed by Honest People

Another challenge presented by security systems in general is that they're designed by honest people to stop mostly professional, creative, and well-prepared perpetrators. This approach has an embedded contradiction, a double-edged sword. Yes, of course we would like honest people to design our security systems–trustworthy people who would not give away their knowledge, take advantage of the system, or cross lines altogether. But honest people do not think like perpetrators and criminals. Though we think we do, we lack the daring, imagination, and at times the malice driving their thinking.

Moreover, honest people developing security concepts are parts of large teams, companies, or government. They are fulfilling their jobs by applying *their* knowledge, experience and understanding in an attempt to meet their superiors' directives, human rights, and other legal issues. Thus, security designers are not free to choose what they think is a good solution, they need also need to pass the scrutiny of bosses and their ideas, lawyers, and even operational experts. Thus, on top of struggling with internal and external limitations, a designer needs to think like a perpetrator. As it is very hard to mentally enter and play the role of the lone, money- or ideology-driven perpetrator, chances are that honestly designed security systems will have unthought-of back doors.

Years ago, I was invited to participate in a think tank set up by the Ministry of Homeland Security (as it would be called today) of a certain developed country. The think tank, which was led by the Chief Scientist of the office, included professors, police commanders, technologists, and other thinkers whose goal was to devise a way to electronically mark and identify all vehicles to register their locations throughout the country. The data would then help investigate crimes. Putting myself in the perpetrator's position, I thought the solution useless because as a perpetrator, I could drive through side roads or fields, remove or falsify license plates, or steal a car altogether. The concept was great to find out where honest people are, but useless in terms of apprehending perpetrators.

In addition to honesty, there is a need to quickly adapt to changing circumstances and threats presented by ever-changing perpetrators and targets. Such adaptation is unlikely to happen quickly enough by someone who is honest at heart. And if this seems like a moral or philosophical argument, then bear with me, for it is not.

Perpetrators and terrorists are like flowing water, always finding a way to achieve their goals. Block the flow of water with a dam, and the water will find an alternate path. Close the crack, and you have a new one. Mend the leak, and it is just a matter of time until a new one appears. Depending on how high or wide that dam is, water will find less difficult paths; nature is our teacher on this. Similarly, the level of security enacted will determine how difficult it is for perpetrators and terrorists to find alternate means to achieve their goals, be that against a specific site or target, or moving on to an alternative target with similar impact. They *will* find an alternative path. Finding that path in the face of strong security requires a more determined, creative,[8] and better-prepared perpetrator like the drug lords of South America.

These drug lords began smuggling drugs into the US in cargo trucks by land, then moved to using tunnels and ships, to using cannons to shoot drug shipments across the border fence.[9] They then shifted to using underwater barrels towed by boats or ships. They even use small, self-made submarines. And yet, still, we cannot block all shipments. In the words of Marine General John F. Kelly, commander, US Southern Command, giving testimony at a hearing before the US Senate:[10]

> Last year, we had to cancel more than 200 very effective engagement activities in numerous multilateral exercises. Because of asset shortfalls, we're unable to get after 74 percent of suspected maritime drug trafficking. I simply sit and watch it go by. And, because of service cuts, I don't expect to get any immediate relief, in terms of assets to work with in this

---

[8] http://edition.cnn.com/2009/CRIME/04/16/creative.drug.smugglers/

[9] http://world.time.com/2013/03/02/marijuana-by-air-mexican-gangs-use-cannon-to-hurl-drugs-across-u-s-border/

[10] Committee on Armed Services, Thursday, March 13, 2014, p. 6 http://www.armed-services.senate.gov/imo/media/doc/14-21%20-%203-13-14.pdf See more at: http://www.drugwarfacts.org/cms/Drug_Interdiction#sthash.p82a4ENs.dpuf

region of the world. Ultimately, the cumulative impact of our reduced engagement won't be measured in the number of cancelled activities and reduced deployments; it will be measured in terms of U.S. influence, leadership, relationships in a part of the world where our engagement has made a real and lasting difference over the decades.

Honest people designing security installations is a good thing, but the truth is that whatever systems are designed, perpetrators simply come up with ever more creative ways of surmounting these obstacles, ways that honest designers in massive organizations may not imagine or predict and may lack the flexibility to deal with. The result is that we amend the corral after the horses have escaped; we keep developing solutions to meet past experience and not future potential attacks. We have become followers, not leaders.

The Interface or Boundary Problem

Any complex system or organization has many interfaces, elements of the organization that must communicate and cooperate with each other. These interfaces may be, for example, between security units that cover adjacent areas, between field units and their superiors who aren't in the field, between superiors and commanders, or between field units and intelligence sources. When an event occurs and chaos is all around, these interfaces, their communication and coordination are put to the ultimate test.

The most critical interface here is that between security agents and suspicious elements (people, objects, or wares), because it is the first, and sometimes last, line of defense. It is where detection takes place and first responders react. This interface requires sharp detection skills, profiling, and intuition, as well as the ability to respond quickly to prevent and contain the situation. Slow reactions normally end in the perpetrator's success or in a rolling event like the San Bernardino or Orlando terror attacks.

An example involving such an interface problem is that of the Nigerian Umar Farouq Abdulmutallab, known as the "Underwear Bomber." On Christmas Day 2009, he attempted to detonate a bomb on Northwest Airlines Flight 253 from Amsterdam to Detroit.

Abdulmutallab was indoctrinated by extreme Islamists, including the American Yemeni Muslim preacher Anwar al-Awlaki, who is implicated in several high-profile attacks, including the 2009 Fort Hood shooting and 9/11. Abdulmutallab publicly discussed his opinions, even posting on Facebook his support of jihad and hatred to the West and capitalism. In May 2009, the UK Border Agency denied his visa application, placing his name on the security watch list because of immigration fraud rather than for a security reason. This information was not shared with other Western agencies.

On November 19, Abdulmutallab's father spoke with two CIA officers in Abuja, Nigeria, reporting his son's "extreme religious views" and telling the embassy that Abdulmutallab might be in Yemen. Thus, Abdulmutallab's name was added to the US's 550,000-name Terrorist Identities Datamart Environment, a database of the National Counterterrorism Center (NCTC). But his name was not added to any FBI or No Fly watch lists. In addition, his American visa was not revoked because of intelligence officials' request claiming that revoking Abdulmutallab's visa would disrupt a larger investigation into Al-Qaeda.

The conclusion is that certain interfaces did not work properly. UK did not share the suspicion of "immigration fraud," and the CIA did not share their suspicions with the FBI, which controls the No-Fly lists. With today's technology, the transfer of such information requires no effort; what does require an effort is the mapping and implementation of such interfaces and links.

Another such example is the TSA's failure[11] to identify 73 of their *own* employees who had links to terrorism. A 2015 report from the Department of Homeland Security inspector general found that this "oversight" was due to lack of interagency communication.

Such interfaces are also measured in terms of time, like how early do we provide intelligence or detect the threat, how quickly do we react upon it and, how rapidly do we move the information to supporting elements like calling reinforcements

---

[11] "TSA Fails to ID 73 Airport Employees With Links to Terrorism," Halimah Abdullah. http://www.nbcnews.com/news/us-news/tsa-fails-identify-73-employees-terror-watch-lists-n371601

and Red-Cross. Interfaces are in communications, language, "handshakes." All need to be thought of and revised even if the conclusion is that nothing needs to be changed.

The challenge of detecting and preventing security breaches, and improving the critical interface between agents and suspicious elements, is where we turn next.

Improving the Critical Interface

In order to improve said interface between security agents and suspicious elements, there are four central aspects to be considered.

As discussed, the transition between "normal" mode and "emergency" mode happens in close to zero time–the time it takes to realize a threat is present. It is in this transition that first responders need to successfully detect, block, and contain the event or potential threat. First responders must be mentally and intellectually prepared to cope with scenarios that can and do change by the minute. Courage, focus, and mental flexibility are put to the test. Attempts to mechanize responses and thinking result in the loss of that intangible flexibility that helps catch perpetrators off guard with an unexpected response that may confuse them thus transferring the initiative to the first responder, who now holds the "element of surprise" rather than the perpetrator himself holding it.

Fixed and static security installations are large machines attempting to identify individuals or small groups of flexible perpetrators. This is sort of like expecting big government to operate like a startup company. We are imposing a static obstacle on those dynamic and flexible perpetrators who not only surprise us, but who are used to improvising under changing conditions. This is a challenge to be considered.

Maintaining 100% alertness and vigilance 24/7 is impossible. Surprise checks in US airports have proven this is the case, partially because of staff profiles, but also because of technology limitations or flaws, un-calibrated equipment, and limited equipment performance. It is known as a fact that many potential threats are not detected, calling for constant revision and site-specific thinking. One personal experience is when I witnessed three impatient youngsters skipping a JFK security check queue by entering undetected through a personnel exit. From their body language and glances, it was clear to me they were looking to jump the queue; thus, any agent could have detected and prevented this.

Alertness, awareness, and mental flexibility are needed to cope with constantly changing conditions, threats, crowds, and perpetrator profiles. And yet security personnel are instructed to follow procedures rather than be flexible, and are educated that their superiors are their bosses, when in fact it is the perpetrators who are their bosses, who practically determine how and when staff should react. Here again, I experienced a TSA agent so busy complaining about her superior officer that she, because of my empathy toward her, failed to check me properly. Her emotions affected her judgment, something that shouldn't happen and yet did. Another example is that of an off-duty Santa Monica police officer who boarded a flight to Taiwan with a gun that made it past airport security. TSA officials said, "standard procedures were not followed."[12]

Improvement of this critical interface between security agent and potential perpetrator requires strengthening the "human factor," increase their preparedness for the unexpected and improve their reaction against it. Naturally, surprises catch people off guard; they shock and confuse us. But we can train to improve on this, to help us expect the unexpected. Consider the following factors that affect detection and reaction outcomes:

- Behavior of both personnel and the person being checked. Perhaps someone slept badly, had a quarrel with their spouse, or is stressed about an important business trip (or, similarly, is stressed because they're carrying contraband). Heightened awareness of behavior patterns quite simply aids detection;

- Operators are not always aware of equipment drawbacks and their very specific functionality, making them rely on machines beyond their engineered capabilities. Obviously, this is simply a matter of education, ensuring that operators know what equipment is capable of and opening their minds to detect what equipment doesn't

---

[12] http://edition.cnn.com/2017/04/20/politics/tsa-gun-lax-taiwan/index.html

detect, like 3D-printed guns that cannot be detected by metal detectors;

- To combat the finite and limited nature of procedures, it is necessary to train people to have mental flexibility so that they react within the wider spirit of the directives rather than following them to the letter. Written procedures and training are for staff to follow, yet terror and crime do not follow "our" rule book. Thus, superiors must trust agents and relieve them from the need to ask for "permission" to make on-the-spot decisions, personnel should be allowed to react per the specific situations *within the spirit* of the general directives;

A further but higher level of interface is that between field agents and intelligence sources. The more information a security agent has, the better he or she can prepare and act on it. Receiving prior intelligence, even on seemingly unconnected things such as pro-environment organizations infiltrating nuclear power stations, helps. Communication lines and personal trust need to be there, and intelligence bodies need to be educated that more intelligence is often better than none. That said, to much intelligence can become counterproductive.

Ensuring the quality and sustainability of this critical agent-perpetrator, intelligence-detection-reaction interface is extremely important in meeting the challenges of detecting and preventing criminal and terrorist activities. But let us now take this information and move with it to a more concrete explanation of HLS specifically, starting with a look at HLS from a managerial standpoint.

HLS from a Managerial Standpoint

The qualitative aspects of management are
where the seeds of success or failure are sown.

The goal of Homeland Security is to protect our way of life and the values that define it. This role is fulfilled by governments–whether democracies, dictatorships, or totalitarian regimes–who work to protect themselves, both internally and externally. HLS is the interface between internal and external protection, protecting the tangible and intangible, physical and information "borders" of our way of life and our government. Borders, of course, have entry and exit points used mainly by law-abiding citizens. But the complexity of HLS's work begins with backdoors, those unofficial, undefined crossing points. HLS's job is made even more complex by the wide-ranging motivations of perpetrators, as already mentioned. After all, rules and laws are there for the masses to follow and for the rest to exploit. Therefore, managing the combination of said entries and exits–which are varied, long, and form a complex interface–is extremely challenging.

Security is about "understanding the market," namely: the perpetrators and risks, which are diverse. And, like in any organization, the challenges further increase when cultural, religious, or language gaps are involved. Each people-group: folk, gang, ethnicity, etc. on the globe has a culture, tradition, religion, and history, which take them forward and for which they are willing to fight. The developed world has its culture and values, which, as stated, it seeks to protect. But to succeed, we must also understand perpetrator cultures so that the extent of determination, cruelty, and opportunism can be evaluated and prepared for. We have seen this with drug lords murdering whole families or parts of villages, bribes, threats, and ridding themselves of corpses using acids. Since 9/11 we have seen the extent of imaginative cruelty extreme Islamists are willing to exercise to murder "infidels." We see the torture, murder, slavery, sexual abuse, and other crimes ISIS is committing in the name of Islam. We are appalled, while for them, terrorists and criminals alike, these are the "commandments" to follow. Failure to understand such cultural differences strongly affects our ability to win the HLS war. It is a form of negotiation, the pre-boxing-fight dance in which knowing and feeling your opponent is crucial. It is about the intangibles, not about ticking checklists.

Another aspect is the financial one. Our perpetrators, having the initiative and exploiting the surprise factor, have the advantage of using far smaller and more agile organizations with better-prepared people. Their costs are marginal to negligible compared to governmental investments in protecting against them. Criminals and terrorists can buy materials in any shop and assemble bombs, connect them to a detonator, and then blow up their targets. Their cost is low, and impact can be very big in terms of lives, assets, and public opinion. A specific example of cost imbalance is that of Israel's "Iron Dome" air defense system developed to counter Hamas's rockets frequently shot over to Israel. Every Hamas rocket costs a few hundred dollars to make, while the development and deployment of Iron Dome cost a few billion US dollars, and each missile costs tens of thousands of US dollars. The justification for such investment is the cost of damage vs. cost of defense, rather than perpetrator weapon costs vs. cost of our counter solution. The return on security investment is therefore measured using the same currency the perpetrator does–lives and damage.

The next challenge is the operational one: the concept and execution of how to detect and prevent such malicious activities from affecting our way of life. There are many types of managerial theories and structures of both civilian and military origin that are applicable to HLS routine processes where we seek to optimize detection and prevent negative results, while minimizing the impact on our daily lives.

Most HLS resources are dedicated to fixed locations and crossing points (static), while a smaller portion is dedicated to "special events" and unofficial, dynamic routes. Because of the quantity and variety of people, valuables, and goods (legal or illegal) that wish to enter and exit areas under the purview of HLS, the managerial challenges here are quite immense. Putting together an organization that can effectively apply HLS in such widely varying environments and situations requires creativity, special measures, and adaptation to local and regional risks, weather, and culture. This is achieved through localization of solutions and extremely effective coordination with bordering regions, adjacent forces, and intelligence.

But the success of such HLS organizations depends first and foremost on people, particularly leadership. Good, focused, people-oriented leadership with a wide understanding of said challenges, adversaries, cultures, and mitigation means will achieve good results. Leaders who focus on form rather than essence will not only lose their staff's motivation, daring, and imagination–ending up with poor results–but will also fail to identify the ever-changing threats.

Experience shows that the closer leaders are to their regions and the more authority they are given to make their own decisions, the better the results. As leadership moves further away from the field, it should strengthen and encourage local leadership to accept and live up to their new challenge. Failure to do so results in slow and failed activities like in the case of FEMA during Hurricane Katrina, discussed in more detail in chapter 6.

At times, form plays a greater role; leaders meddle with details instead of leadership and strategic issues, deflecting attention from *why* security is there to *how* to execute it. Great execution of a poor strategy will yield far inferior results than mediocre execution of a strong strategy.

The Managerial Challenge

Before we get further into the issues of HLS, let's first discuss the managerial challenge and the elements of managing any HLS organization, both of which inevitably lead us to the human factor and its leadership.

Which Managerial Approach Works for HLS?

Essentially, HLS works like any other process such as chemical plants, oil refineries, or even restaurants. Since the seventeenth century, over three hundred and sixty different management theories have been developed, from Adam Smith's scientific approach to today's Theory of Constraints. There is also an abundance of military strategies and tactical theories developed over generations, from China's Sun Tzu to Germany's von Clausewitz and the Englishman B.H. Liddell Hart; like attrition warfare, divide and conquer, battle of annihilation, blockade or siege, deception, and distraction–to name a few.

Which of these theories is best recommended for HLS? The answer to that is "none." There is no one-size-fits-all option here, and like with every human-dependent organization, leadership, through its personality and choices, defines and practically develops the security-and-management theory to be used. Good leaders do so bringing a deep understanding of the challenges, people, and tools they have; they apply them with creativity and cunning while leveraging the experience of others including some of said theories. It is these leaders whose results we then praise and study upon success.

Because HLS forces are security forces, their leadership tends to adopt a chain of command, a centralized managerial (command) approach. But, unlike police forces or armies, the role of HLS is defensive and static because HLS agents act within defined perimeters. They do not chase suspects outside of a protected perimeter, away from the crossing points they are responsible for, beyond airport limits, or inland when criminals cross the border. They are more like bodyguards whose job it is to remove their VIP from harm's way, not to fight the perpetrators unless it is necessary. Police and FBI do the tracing, tracking and chasing until perpetrator's apprehension.

As stated, HLS organizations are different from other security forces in that agents are subject to so much variability. Each agent in each one of her or his shifts can detect and prevent malicious events, or miss that fatal threat. According to publications about ECHELON and 9/11, critical information was missed by humans who operated the system, missed by the people who defined words and phrases to look for or to be translated, not by the technology itself. And, unless additional detection circles exist, there are no real second chances.

HLS agents can be anyone involved: the technician calibrating systems, the operator of these systems, the control-

50

center agent, the field agent looking the passenger in the eye, or the one watching the X-ray scanner display. While police forces, emergency organizations, and armies are built with several layers of support and command, HLS practically depends solely on first line agents. Yes, those agents may use technology, but they are still the epicenter of the organization. They are the all-important human factor.

In hierarchical, normally rigid, execution-only organizations, decisions are made at the top, and field agents are to execute them. Most large, especially HLS-related organizations tend to adopt this model because of the afore-discussed notion of predictable results. All agents in position X do A, and all those in Y do B. This rigid approach can be successful only if additional intangible and soft-skill elements are added to agents' performance to ensure that coverage also exists between agents X and Y and activities A and B. Lack of soft skills reduces rigid organizations into instances where the means become the goal and the soul is missing.

An opposite approach to HLS rigid command is a Decentralized or Distributed Management approach as used in the most successful companies and organizations, particularly those that depend highly on the human factor, on human abilities and motivation. This approach is also used in some military and paramilitary units where high-level goals are given to a unit whose responsibility includes planning, training, and equipping itself. The success of such units is based on intensive training that develops personal and professional trust in peers and confidence that they are up to the task. Your life may depend on your peers' professionalism.

At its simplest, Distributed Management moves authority and responsibility downward, onto those leading the task at hand. It requires good people, independent leaders, and motivated team players, who build a chain of trust from those at the top to local leadership to agents in the field. Moreover, by having local leadership plan location-specific solutions, local factors are considered such as topography, flora and fauna, cultural differences, seasons, habits, or extraordinary behaviors. In addition, such ownership increases leadership and team motivation to prove that their way works and they are worthy of the trust given to them. The flexibility given here to meet individual challenges is what makes this approach such a valuable one for HLS organizations.

Goals and Focus

Managing any organization requires a continuous focus on achieving its goals, in our discussion it is public security. For different reasons, the goals are diluted by micro management defocusing personnel from their real goal. We often see security personnel delay impatient passengers, when almost empty perfume bottles or toys are confiscated or when security agents drag paying and seated passengers off aircraft to make free a seat for a company employee. We would not call a paramedic nor a police officer for such non-issues, so why call on a security agent?

This 'educational' role assumed by security agents implies that their mental attention is in the wrong place. It is up to management and leadership to ensure attention is consistently focused on security only as discussed throughout this book.

Managerial Elements

HLS is planned, built, managed, and maintained, just like any other organization or company. It has strategies and tactics that are developed, implemented, reviewed, and periodically updated, particularly after a crisis has occurred. Like factories, higher capital investment in HLS increases throughput, not necessarily creating better results. Unlike factories, staffing does not necessarily shrink with increased capital investments, nor does security improve with overstaffing.

Unlike businesses and some other security forces, HLS is reactive, in that it must react to suspects, their individual and group profiles, to illegal goods, threatening situations, intelligence, warnings, and the like. Also, unlike most businesses, HLS has no real measurable profit and loss; it is simply there, much like the mostly transparent office cleaner who is noticed only when absent. HLS is a must in our world, and, naturally, we seek to minimize the organization's interference with the natural flow of people, information, finances, and goods, thus lessening HLS's interference with our daily activities. But here, just as in business, "clients," or we - travelers, expect short delivery (screening) times; accessible pricing, which is added as security fees to transportation tickets; port fees on cargo (eventually, we tax payers pick up the bill); and service reliability (true prevention).

Procedures are an essential operations-management element in most companies. In HLS, these also seek to define responses to events and workable plans which are unable to cover the infinite range of possible threats, behaviors, risks, and reactions involved. Counter to industry, sticking to HLS procedures inevitably reduces quality of detection, leaves security voids, and even causes confusion when an event outside the scope of procedures occurs. Therefore, out-of-the-box thought flexibility and expecting the unexpected should be adopted in HLS just like in the successful high-technology industries.

On the other hand, any attempt to increase the amount and detail of procedures to cover all eventualities will backfire. Overburdening agents with such procedures will deem procedures useless, simply because of the human factor. People are unable to remember intensely detailed protocols, may remember or understand them differently from what the writer intended, and may even fail to act as procedures dictate in emergency. All this leads once more to the conclusion that the most essential managerial elements for HLS organizations must account for the human factor in trusting it, motivating it, and training it, particularly training for the unexpected, which makes the difference between success and failure in an HLS setting. But trusting field agents and their judgment practically neutralizes procedures. The challenge is therefore to balance between trusting our agents in the different security agencies and still have them operate along guidelines set by procedures.

The Human Factor

The human factor is an integral part of any organization including HLS, but it is also an inherent problem, one that must be addressed. Human interactions in security are key to successful results, all the way from those inter-agency interfaces to communication between agents in the field. Efficacy and effectiveness of such cooperation depends only on people. We decide which communication lines will be open; we decide which intelligence and databases will be shared, the actions, reactions, and their quality. Opening the managerial scope to allow cooperation between different security bodies is critical. Such interfaces are all about people whose good will, passions, determination, fears, and egos define how specific, effective, and fast cooperation is. But history is rich with mistrust, with ego wars that result in flushing the baby with the bathwater, situations where ultimate goals are sacrificed for lesser, individual goals. This goes all the way down to field agents, who, for example, may take the initiative and react jointly and coherently to an event or "play by the book" and assume someone else will react. Thus, both would do nothing, allowing the perpetrator to continue his or her actions.

There are ways to minimize negative effects of the human factor and its outcomes, but first let us have a more detailed look at specific aspects of the human factor.

Leadership Defining HLS and Priorities

The human factor is all over: policymakers, leaders, heads of forces, executives of protected assets, designers, planners, employees, security agents... in short–everybody. Some of these people affect future potential threats; others the priority of threats; choice of technologies and equipment, staff, or training; and some affect the way that actual security checks are performed. The HLS process is inescapably intertwined with the human factor, with all the pros and cons it entails.

Heads of state, through their political and personal policies, define levels of risk. For example, Europe invites Muslim immigrants to enter, and amongst those immigrants are a small number of extremists whose mission is to further the Islamic Jihad. Think of Berlin 2016, where a Muslim refugee, welcomed by Germany, murdered a semi-trailer truck driver and crashed the truck into a Christmas market, killing 12 and wounding 48. The heads of state are the ones who need to understand cultures and motivations to better assess potential outcomes of their decisions. This, of course, is easier said than done, as a quick historical example shows. Neville Chamberlain, then prime minister of the United Kingdom, signed the notorious Munich Agreement in 1938 with the understanding that Nazi Germany would be allowed to annex parts of then Czechoslovakia in return for peace and the halting of further German expansionist claims. This led to the Russian-German Molotov-Ribbentrop non-aggression pact of 1939. Both agreements were violated at the convenience of the German Nazi government, exposing Chamberlain's inability to understand his adversary. The leader of the PLO, Yasser Arafat, signed a peace agreement with Israel at the White House in 1993, and though he praised the agreement in English, in Arabic he referred to it as the Hudaybiyyah Pact, a peace agreement signed between Muhammad and the Quraysh tribe of Mecca that the prophet violated two years later. Arafat hinted that he would violate the peace agreement at his convenience, just like the Prophet Muhammad did. Similarly, agreements with North Korea and Iran are being violated, the two nations like teenagers, testing their limits with no reaction from the nations that countersigned the agreements.

It is the politicians, the heads of state and their like, who take a leading role here. They must understand their adversary (be that ISIS, Iran, Venezuela, or North Korea) or partner, his culture, agenda, and motivations. More than once we have seen that this does not always happen. Policies and their impact define potential threats, those policies defined by decision makers and think tanks alike. Policies are also biased by human drives, wishes, gut feelings, egos, and hatreds, as seen with President George W. Bush's campaign to justify the 2003 invasion of Iraq. Such human biases will be discussed later in more detail.

Choosing the most probable and critical threats to be protected against is also biased by people, their cultures, and education, affecting the quality and scope of threat identification, detection, and mitigation. Condoleezza Rice, national security advisor during the 9/11 attacks, stated that no one could have imagined that there was a goal of hijacking planes and crashing them into the World Trade Center and the Pentagon. The question should have been whether a terrorist cell was organizing itself and converging at a certain time or date to attack targets on US soil, information that arguably could have been found out. This theme of "fantastical" attacks is illustrated throughout history in the examples discussed in Chapter 2, by the likes of Napoleon at the Battle of Austerlitz, Hannibal crossing the Alps, and the Trojan Horse. We know that the fantastical can happen and must be considered and kept in mind when planning for contingencies. Our leaders must be creative no matter how unreasonable a chance there may be of something happening.

The General Findings sections of the Final Report of the National Commission on (9/11) Terrorist Attacks Upon the United States[13] begins by stating:

Since the plotters were flexible and resourceful, we cannot know whether any single step or series of steps would have defeated them. What we can say with confidence is that none of the measures adopted by the U.S. government from 1998 to 2001 disturbed or even delayed the progress of the al Qaeda plot. Across the government, there were failures of imagination, policy, capabilities, and management.

The next section named "Imagination" continues:

---

[13] http://govinfo.library.unt.edu/911/report/911Report_Exec.htm

The most important failure was one of imagination. We do not believe leaders understood the gravity of the threat. The terrorist danger from Bin Ladin and al Qaeda was not a major topic for policy debate among the public, the media, or in the Congress.

Therefore, leadership is the first to determine HLS priorities and risks; they are the most important human factor whose drives and attitudes influence security results.

Intelligence

An additional aspect in which the human factor influences HLS is intelligence. Intelligence must be collected from all sources, using a variety of means. Intelligence is a key weapon in the HLS's arsenal. Background intelligence can help us understand a perpetrator's culture, motivations, and nuances such as use of language, body language, and typical behaviors. The subsequent interpretation of intelligence should be done using the *perpetrator's* cultural background rather than our own. Operational intelligence is used as a basis for action and reaction, for prevention, and to increase the probability thereof because *forewarned is forearmed.*

The gathering, prioritization, analysis, and sharing of intelligence are also heavily dependent on the human factor. Intelligence is analyzed and understood through one's own cultural biases, it is evaluated through our understanding of the context, and it is prioritized and cross-checked by us. The human factor decides if a piece of valuable information may or may not end up in the right hands because agent decisions are also biased by personality, training, colleagues, and superiors. Once it has been decided that information is of value, it must be moved as quickly as possible to the field, avoiding ego games, competitiveness, pretexts of vacation and travel, and other human behaviors that delay propagation of intelligence.

Intelligence misinterpretation, biased analysis or delayed dissemination translate into deficiencies in intelligence, priorities, its contextual understanding and conclusions. Intelligence is then lost from those that need it most, when they need it most, be these leaders, decision makers, or field agents. There are ways of reducing these gaps of understanding by filtering, prioritizing, and overcoming personality issues. Examples include think tanks that counter conclusions, brainstorming and invoking a deeper and wider analysis of information and a more "open-minded" approach. By listening to those whom no one wants to listen to, we create dissonance and challenge people to think. Think of pre-9/11 incriminating messages intercepted by ECHELON that were translated[14] only after the event because of wrong priorities, and priorities are set by people even when programmed into a computer.

Somewhere, someone must analyze, conclude, dare, and decide, strongly impacting HLS results.

---

[14] "NSA Intercepts on Eve of 9/11 Sent a Warning - Messages Translated After Attacks," Walter Pincus and Dana Priest, *Washington Post* staff writers. http://echelononline.free.fr/documents/wp_20062002.htm

Perpetrators

We have already discussed perpetrators in the preceding chapter, so I will not dwell on the topic here. However, we must keep in mind that perpetrators themselves–with their differing motivations, methods, cultures, biases, and behavior–are yet another human factor in the HLS equation. Perpetrators are just as likely to affect HLS results as HLS agents themselves are, and they suffer just as much from human deficiencies as HLS agents do. The weakness of one is the opportunity of the other, with perpetrators having the advantage of collecting intelligence and having the initiative and surprise factors on their side.

Defensive and Detecting Staff

From top-level decision makers to perpetrators, intelligence people, and commanders, the last link in the human chain is the HLS front-line staff and employees. While others are behind the scenes making more high-level or theoretical decisions, field agents are facing real threats head on, making these agents one of the most critical components in HLS because:

- Generally, they have one opportunity to detect a perpetrator or malicious device;

- They are the first detectors *and* the first responders;

- Their alertness and motivation must allow them to identify not only the expected threats but also unexpected ones as well;

- In lack of preliminary information, they are to find the unknown and unexpected needle in one of many haystacks.

Field agents are the face of HLS and are exposed to heroic actions just as they are prone to terrible failures. They have the most noticeable influence on the tactical success of HLS organizations.

We have spoken of human deficiencies that affect the effectiveness of HLS organizations, for which we compensate by increasing the use of consistent and accurate technology. But, as stated, technology is inflexible, reduces staff alertness, and is costly to replace or upgrade. In some cases, the use of technology reflects a latent mistrust in people, leading to increased spending on equipment and less on empowering good people, resulting in a de-facto preference for people quantity over investing in their abilities. But in practice, better people minimize risks, connect remote dots, offer more comprehensive detection capabilities, and complement the limited equipment performance. People, not the equipment, are first responders. The challenge, therefore, is to find good professionals–a difficult task in normally low-paid, motivation-lacking jobs.

This dependency on the human factor dictates a need for higher trust, for a Distributed Management system, because a rigid and hierarchical organization shifts employee attention from the mission at hand to obeying the rules, from security considerations to operational ones. It is unfair to expect field agents to fulfill their role when bound by hierarchy and procedures that narrow their intellectual and sensory freedom like eye blinders limiting a racehorse's field of view.

Let us translate the above into staffing issues in HLS.

The Staffing Oxymoron

The staffing of HLS has become somewhat of an oxymoron. To standardize and unify responses and their predictability, we mechanize organizations through training, procedures, the expropriation of decision making, and tight controls. Staff members are turned into parts of a great machine. For some, this is good; for others, it imposes restrictions that may or may not be necessary. But what happens if an event is beyond the scope of the originally designed and implemented "machine"? Who has the authority to make decisions not covered by procedures, and how long should teams wait for such decisions? Waiting for decisions, especially from off-site command, may be deadly, while taking initiative is practically forbidden, leaving a void exploited by resourceful perpetrators.

The dilemma is defining the fine line between the machine serving the goal and the machine becoming the (latent) goal. Do we always put detection and prevention as our goal, or sometimes do we focus on process and form, neglecting the reason security is there to begin with? If procedures, mechanization, and operating technology are the priority, we lose the human touch, that touch that can detect extraordinary human behaviors. If we want to re-humanize the machine, we need to encourage agents to look at people, let them make independent judgments to handle real-time, local cases and events. In corporations, this works; companies with distributed and coordinated decision making are more efficient and successful like Google and Apple.

Can this be done with HLS? Yes. Should it be done? Yes. This is the only way to enable a more effective overall response, namely detection of the unexpected and unknown, reaction, action, and containment, especially of event scenarios not previously experienced. For example: if there is a shooter in a building, guards may be given the option to neutralize the shooter, as opposed to a protocol-based reaction in which the shooter is blocked or contained in a specific area until SWAT teams arrive. In the first scenario, the shooting may be stopped immediately or drawn away from innocent people; in the second scenario, the shooting continues until the SWAT team arrives on the scene. Yes, SWATs are more professional and will, from the moment of their arrival, conclude the event in a shorter time and with less (additional) casualties. But maybe the guards on duty can conclude the event immediately with a *lower* total number of casualties, as could have been the case in Paris's Bataclan, where, according to the New York Times:[15]

> The first officer to reach the worst of the carnage–
> *at the Bataclan concert hall*, where 90 of the 130
> victims that night were killed–got there roughly

---

[15] http://www.nytimes.com/2016/01/01/world/europe/response-to-paris-attacks-points-to-weaknesses-in-french-police-structure.html?_r=0

15 minutes into the attack. Armed with only a service sidearm, he managed to stall the killing by shooting one attacker, blowing up the terrorist's suicide vest while sparing the victims around him.

Yet the officer was ordered to withdraw in favor of a more specialized antiterrorism unit, which arrived half an hour into the assault after initially being sent to sites where the violence had already ended. Another specialized unit nearby was apparently never deployed, according to a French news report.

Of course, this management style can only work with the right staffing, which brings us to the inherent contradictions with current staffing policies.

Slow-Moving Agents Against Quick, Creative Perpetrators
Motivation

As with any other organization, HLS can be no better than the people who form it, particularly considering our conclusion that the human factor has the largest impact on positive outcomes. The better leadership, managers or commanders, and field agents are, the better results will be. More threats will be detected and mitigated. And yet today's staffing represents in many HLS organizations a quantitative compromise rather than the meeting of a high-level qualitative goal.

Improving staff performance is not only an issue of salary,

though in some cases it may be. There are other factors as well. Motivation, team cohesion, open communications, treatment by superiors, and other such human-related factors can help improve performance and results, including of those who join for lack of better employment alternatives.

In many organizations staff is not motivated or effective. When crossing borders, we may find alert customs agents. Yet in airports we find overloaded TSA agents who miss passengers sneaking through security, entering from a staff exit; good-will use of machinery without understanding its impact on detection. We also find disgruntled agents overwhelmed with their boss's attitude so they are too busy complaining to focus on their work. On the other end of the spectrum, we find agents going strictly by the book to the point of absurdity, confiscating an almost empty bottle of aftershave lotion. And these are just some of my personal experiences.

The Real-Time Test

We see a man leaning under the hood of a car and think to ourselves, "Oh, the poor guy's car broke down." We rarely think that we are witnessing a car theft in progress. Or we hear house alarms go off and do nothing despite our neighbor's house being emptied.

In case of a real security event, which agents need to identify as such, they also need to shift mind and body from a mechanical routine to 100% alertness, thinking, identifying, and responding. Under the given conditions, it is hardly surprising that staff members in many HLS organizations are not the fastest to think, detect, and react, or the best at understanding that a threat is right in front of them. And yet these people are the first detectors and first responders. They are the ones who will need to switch from a tedious routine to a focused reaction in no time at all, from TSA routine to jumping on and neutralizing a terrorist with a strap-on bomb, as in the March 2016 attack in the Brussels Airport. Can these people be replaced with young, well-trained, highly motivated employees? Can they be trained to become elite HLS units? Probably not.

What can be done is to focus their persona, attention, mind, and soul to detecting threats, enhancing their judgment and self-confidence, helping them perceive and profile people. They will not neutralize the terrorist, but they will alert police and the public. In short, their performance can be improved, and I dare think that when trusted and entrusted, it will.

Security agents need to be given the flexibility to respond in an appropriate manner to threats. As President Gerald Ford expressed it:

> "Our constitution works. Our great republic is a
> government of laws, not of men."

Or in security language, procedures and form override people and goals. But, as already discussed, procedures are finite, just like laws, which are not singular for every felony and scope, leaving the law's interpretation and application to courts of law. Similarly, HLS procedures, as important as they are, should be used as guidelines rather than directives to be followed to the letter. This is especially true considering that threats sometimes change much faster than the speed at which procedures can be adapted, updated, and diffused to all agents. Field agents are people and should be treated as such, allowing them the same freedom to be creative and adapt to situations as perpetrators have when exercising their malice. This will create a more even playing field.

Interbody and Interagency Cooperation

Every government has several security organizations focused on public security and safety, each with a specific responsibility. HLS depends on information, alerts, and support from peer security organizations pointing at expected, potential, upcoming, or rolling events, allowing local teams to prepare, shut down critical processes, close institutions, close airports, and apply other defensive measures.

While this open sharing of information between agencies sounds good in theory, in many instances information is not shared at all. This happens for a variety of reasons, from wrong prioritization, ego, and credit wars to not wanting to reveal sources, mistrust in keeping information confidential, or simple oversights. Not sharing critical information may prove disastrous like prior to the 9/11 events, when several tip-offs were given to the CIA, including the names of some of the terrorists. Some of that information was not shared with the FBI,[16]

---

[16] "They Tried to Warn Us: Foreign Intelligence Warnings Before 9/11," Paul Thompson.

who failed to probe deeper into those names. Yes, the intelligence agencies were exhausted by "over-warning." Thus, priorities were missed, also impacting proper analysis of information gathered by the ECHELON COMINT system. Similarly, the *USS Cole*, bombed by terrorists while being refueled in Yemen's Aden harbor, was aware of such prior attempts on US ships. Or with Belgium's 2016 airport and metro attacks, or Paris's Bataclan theater attack–and the list goes on of events where, in retrospect, prior information was available.

Decisions and Their Impact

Listen to what is not said.

Decisions are made by people based on the information available at the time those decisions are made. Decisions are made by people using their perception, knowledge, and interpretation of information, but not only. People also cling to comfort zones and are bound by social pressures, expectations, and moods. In many cases, we are the prisoners of the professional and social webs to which our lives are attached and on which we depend. We fear stepping outside of those webs, themselves created by our personality, experience, and environment. Decisions reflect our thinking and clarity, but they are also biased by emotions, egos, passions, love, jealousy, hate, moods, intuition, and fears. Understanding the impact of emotions on conclusions and decisions will help leverage positive biases and suppress misleading ones. Passion, for example, is a driving ingredient for success, but it can also lead to unwanted results.

Every decision has a qualitative root, a gut feeling, a human bias that needs to be identified so that its impact can be assessed. Our gut feelings develop throughout our lives combining our intellect, life experience, know-how, and emotions. Such qualitative decisions can't be quantified unless, as discussed, they are simplified and reduced for quantification purposes. When carefully analyzing the roots of decisions, we will find a spark of a qualitative, gut-based direction that we then seek to justify, rationalize, and formulate as a logic decision. It is not a coincidence that the same security forces or companies, under different leadership, create totally different results. One such example is the metamorphosis NYPD went through under Mayor Rudy Giuliani, who—with the same people but decisive leadership, vision, goal setting, and support—led NYPD to new heights. The difference between Giuliani and previous leadership was the qualitative aspects of his decision making and the state of mind he instilled. Rather than just following protocol, he set measurable parameters (including ways to prioritize different kinds of crime) and supported the police department in achieving the goals that had been set. He instilled an ongoing improvement process to achieve goals, and people had to deliver results.

Another example of a qualitative decision is that of officers or executives who for similar tasks propose different approaches. One wishes to have as many people as possible under his command or management, versus the other, who wants less people but the best people. In the former case, "more" is perceived as powerful, as ability, and as importance; while in the latter, the term "more" is about quality, performance, reaching goals, and results. Different managerial approaches such as this reflect on organizations and their success.

Decisions, decision drivers, the process of decision making, and how decisions are made inarguably affect results in any organization, including HLS.

Decision Making in HLS

There are several levels of decision making in HLS that may vary depending on the actual organization, its scale, the challenges it faces, the importance of protected people or assets, and the probability of attack. The decisions represent a security vision, a "plan of defense," and the scope of reaction and subsequent action. Typically, these decisions would encompass:

- Ongoing identification of changing, risks, threats and potential perpetrators;
- Risk to people, knowledge, and/or assets;
- Geographic spread of these;
- Defensive priorities;
- Development of a mitigation strategy;
- Formulation of operational-level structure and flow;
- Choice of technology to be used;
- Development of procedures;
- Partners and other agencies to cooperate with;

- Profiles of personnel to be hired, their background and training.

The above are some of the human decisions made along a top-down decision tree (from a wide scope down to specifics). But any biased or erroneous decisions made along the way, particularly in earlier stages of the decision-making process such as defining who is the threat and what are his/her potential targets, can deem the entire process or system useless. An error early in the process introduces a continuous, compounded error into the rest of the decision-making process. This may be a result of underestimating an adversary, not developing detailed understanding of the risks and their impact, or inability to imagine perpetrator scenarios, as shown in the following examples:

- Choice of perpetrators and their threats defines what we are up against, the very foundation of all further decisions made. A change of risk might change solutions;

- Mitigation strategies define how well we can detect and neutralize threats, whether it be at their homes or by a last-resort HLS agent;

- The choice of technology and equipment defines not only where we expect to have reliable detection and accurate responses, but also how narrow and specialized that capability is, normally overlooking the already mentioned voids inherent to the inflexibility of each technology;

- The level of personnel and their response under duress. Their ability to react correctly will affect the outcome of any security plan.

We may tick boxes and fill out checklists and still miss critical points because we mechanized the process, losing the essence and soul, the intangibles impacting the reason for which security is needed. When adding pebbles to a box, there are still pockets of air; is the box full? No, the pockets can still be filled with sand and then water.

But it is not only the here-and-now, essential decisions that are important when developing or evaluating security concepts; their adaptability is also important. Many things change over time, reflecting on the validity of past decisions: threats change, new critical assets are developed, geopolitical power-games shift, alertness and reaction abilities need updating, and equipment may become useless with the development of new malicious materials and methods. The time-wise fluidity of the sum of factors dictating HLS needs–*requires*–constant vigil, flexible thinking, and organizations to support seamless change and adaptability to our constantly changing environment.

Dilution of the Implementation
The above-described process results in a security vision, a strategy, and high-level and detailed plans. However, an unconscious dilution process occurs throughout the process of converting the vision into specific teams, procedures, and tangible

equipment. With each step, high-level qualitative ideas are converted into more quantitative practical and executable elements. With each such step, a large "cloudy" idea becomes more specific, and in doing so also becomes more limited, more detailed, bringing afloat the advantages, disadvantages, limitations, and strengths of each implementation approach. Converting the high-level qualitative ideas into a quantitative reality entails simplification, minimization and increased resolution to the point of losing the big picture, sometimes forgetting what the master goal was to begin with.

Think of buying a house. We envision a white house with a garden, wooden windows, three bedrooms, whatever. But once we get out into the market, and to keep up with our budget, the need for compromise begins in line with what is realistically available. We choose a red brick house rather than white, get two bedrooms instead of three, or move to the next neighborhood. Some of these compromises are unimportant details, while some may end up affecting gut feelings, how happy you are with your purchase, and how well your new home fulfills your current and future needs. Each reality-imposed compromise ends up diluting your original vision down, and with enough compromises the original vision is lost altogether. The same happens during the HLS decision-making and -implementation process, where we might end up with equipment that has more limited performance than envisioned (like full-body scanners vs. metal-detecting gates), or agents in their 40s and 50s rather than young Marines.

It is therefore important that, after completion of each step during the process of developing and implementing a security system, a sanity check be done vis-à-vis the original ideas and concepts. The sanity check includes both qualitative and quantitative verification, ensuring the reality-driven executables accomplish the goal *and spirit* of the vision.

Dilution of the Actual Vision

Not only may the security implementation be diluted during implementation, but the vision itself may also be diluted. "That is fantasy; it will not happen" may be a response when developing a vision, or even during planning and training stages. But it is clear today that we are unable to make that claim anymore. No one really foresaw the 9/11 scenario, or the San Bernardino school and Orlando bar killings, or Paris, London, Brussels, and Madrid, but they did happen.

Let us look at a wider perspective of this issue. The West perceives itself as liberal, supporting and helping poor countries and immigrants, making such immigrant-executed attacks unthinkable before they happened. We see ourselves as saviors, as helpers; but for many immigrants, we are viewed as condescending, and we are rich because we made them poor. There is no right or wrong Just how one culture perceives another.

Malmö[17] in Sweden became a stronghold of immigrants

---

[17] http://pamelageller.com/2017/01/sweden-crumbling-demands-military-intervention-muslim-mobs-turn-malmo-no-go-zone.html/,

and Islam to the extent that Swedish police refrains from entering certain neighborhoods to avoid "provocations," and local imams call on youngsters "not to befriend unbelievers" yet do nothing to prevent sexual harassment of Swedish women. Short-term thinking in Malmö has led local leadership to prefer silence and avoid social-political unrest over making the hard decisions necessary for long-term stability. Muslim neighborhoods are assumed to be silent if police are refraining from entering them, and yet much is happening beneath this silence. Arms are being stockpiled, extremists are hiding criminals, Sharia law is being enforced, youths are being indoctrinated to extremist viewpoints, and women are being sexually assaulted. Short-term liberal openness is not shared, joined, or repaid by Islamic immigrants, who continue to segregate and complain, with many exploiting the system. Despite having many Moslems who are peace-loving and do want to assimilate, Malmö, as an example, is becoming more and more of a ticking time bomb.

A similar process happens with crime in which whole towns and neighborhoods are controlled by gangs and drug lords, as was and still is the case in Brazil's *favelas*, Mexico's northern areas where whole villages are controlled by drug lords, and New York before Rudy Giuliani's mayorship.

Understanding the cultures from which perpetrators

---

https://www.spectator.co.uk/2016/09/how-sweden-became-an-example-of-how-not-to-handle-immigration/#,

http://www.dailywire.com/news/12466/how-muslim-migration-made-malmo-sweden-crime-michael-qazvini emerge is crucial in preventing our original security vision from being internally diluted. For example, in Libya, Iraq, and many African countries, there is a hierarchy that begins with family, then clan and tribe, and only then (depending on interests and alliances) local and central government. People may, for example, murder wives or sisters suspected of violating family honor, which in itself has a very flexible definition. Family is above all, and family comes first; there is no turning to a government-instituted system to deal with family-related problems. Muammar Gaddafi managed to unify over 100 tribes under his rule to form and stabilize Libya but only through force, bribery, and joint interests. Iraq and Syria, on the other hand, decomposed into sectarian groups like Kurds, Sunnis, Shiites, Alawites, and Yazidis and became killing fields in which "one must belong." You are either with us or against us; there is no neutral ground. Similar social structures exist in many southern Saharan African countries, where narrow interests (of the family, clan, or tribe) are put above those of the majority, of the country or society.

Western social structure is completely different; it is about central government and obeying laws that are (supposedly) for the good of society. This cultural contradiction creates tensions and misunderstandings with immigrants or people in war zones, where attempts to instill democracy contradict an inherent paternal hierarchy. Children of immigrants are exposed to Western principles at school but other ideals at home; they grow up in a culture that wants to help them and yet is conversely seen as being condescending. And so, the seeds are sown for potential disaster.

Understanding this example of cultural and motivational differences should help us grasp what feeds perpetrator creativity and cultural hate, which keep polarizing–more so when immigrants with strong traditions live within Western society yet are born into and required to follow paternal and religious traditions.

A similar discussion is relevant to criminal elements growing in poor neighborhoods, to children whose parents or siblings are drug dealers, alcoholics, or thieves. One grows in an environment that forms personalities and comfort zones.

On September 10, 2001, the suggestion that four planes would be hijacked on American soil and four buildings targeted, that a successful terrorist attack could kill thousands and destroy the Twin Towers in New York, would have been deemed a fantasy. Everything is fantasy until it materializes, but once it has happened, it's too late. We are left to close the stable after the horses have escaped, attempting to prevent something that has already happened, designing procedures to prevent the exact same thing from happening again, when in fact, it won't–at least not in the same way. We decide to react based on the past when we need to be looking at the future; we need to be as creative as the next terrorist or criminal group planning their next move.

The dilution of the security vision happens because of our human biases, past experiences, our comfort zones, and culture, but it also takes place because we are not as daring and creative as perpetrators are. This is an important change that needs to be integrated into thought and planning patterns, isolating them from social pressures and interest groups while focusing on what is "right" in unbiased terms. What is "right" can always be diluted at a later stage.

Leadership and Vision Dilution

Leaders, by the example they set, the language they use, and the actions they order, send a message to citizens and government institutions. Clear and decisive language sends one message, while soft, evasive, and disconnected language sends a different one. Language needs to be backed with respective actions. To exemplify the latter, let us return to the "Underwear Bomber" and politicians' reactions as discussed by Professor John Mueller from the Ohio State University:[18]

> "Janet Napolitano, who had become Director of Homeland Security earlier in the year, maintained that 'once the incident occurred, the system worked'."

We wonder if she would have made the same statement if the plane had exploded in the air and the "system" of first responders was searching for bodies and debris. In addition, many listeners caught on to the last three words, wondering where was *the system* when the bomber boarded the plane.

---

[18] "Case 33: The Underwear Bomber," John Mueller, Ohio State University. http://politicalscience.osu.edu/faculty/jmueller/33UDWR7.pdf

Mueller continues:

Although Napolitano retained her job despite her supposed gaff, another victim of the terrorism episode didn't. Dennis Blair's tenure as Director of National Intelligence included not only this attempt, but the equally unsuccessful Times Square terrorist effort of May 2010 ... as well as the shooting rampage at Fort Hood by a deranged psychiatrist ... that was too much for President Barack Obama, and Blair was fired on May 20, 2010.

The final victim was the American taxpayer who endured a triple blow. First, Blair's experience is likely to further guarantee that any successor, in an understandable desire to protect an important part of his or her anatomy, will be strongly inclined to expend any sum of taxpayer funds, no matter how ill-advised, if there is any chance at all the expenditure will prevent the spender from suffering Blair's fate. Second, Obama ordered an urgent (and therefore expensive) increase–a "surge" and a "race against time" they called it– in the air marshal program. This, even though it was the passengers who successfully handled the underwear threat and even though any air marshals on board would be of no value whatever because they would be seated far away in first class to keep a wary eye on the cockpit door under the almost never-examined assumption that, despite the lessons of the fourth plane on 9/11, a direct replication of that tragedy is remotely possible. And third, the Transportation Security Administration rushed ahead with the deployment of full-body scanners in American airports (however, not initially at least in foreign ones like the one Abdulmutallab used to board his plane) without, it appears, bothering to comply with a Government Accountability Office demand that their cost-effectiveness be evaluated first. Taxpayers are advised that both the scanners and the air marshal program (both of which cost around $1 billion per year) are likely to fail a cost-benefit analysis.

It seems that both Ms. Napolitano and President Obama let their political and survival instincts overtake their judgment: Ms. Napolitano because she wanted to sound positive about something negative, and the president showing "action" irrespective of its sensibility. Now American and worldwide travelers are trapped in an immense system designed to meet historical threats, a system no one has the courage to change, adapt, and reduce if need be, clearly sending a wrong message to first responders and their superiors, clearly distorting the vision and probably the strategy as well.

Decisions Made During HLS Operations

Other than the initial security-planning decision making, there is a second set of reaction-related decisions dealing with how to respond to an event, contain it, and then return to normal operations. The success of these decisions relies on a variety of parameters including the quality of the security teams involved, their personalities, leadership, individual and team preparation, equipment and infrastructure being used, groundwork, coordination, and the ability to make good decisions under pressure.

Yes, these decisions are also affected by said cultural, societal, emotional, and other biases. But they are also affected by moods and stress. Under duress or in an emergency, human reactions are key to success; they are the ultimate test of the reason why HLS is in place to begin with. Success depends on the ability to instantly identify perpetrators and threats, make instant decisions and execute gut-driven reactions as appropriate. Success is the culmination of all the above-discussed issues: staff, visions, decision making, biases, and implementation, whose ultimate result is the fight-or-flight human instinct. If we know how and what to look for, if we are prepared, trained, aware, and have the right personality, we fight. If not, we flee, mentally or physically, leaving a security void.

To summarize, it is the combination of security vision, its strategy, design, implementation, *and* people that make security, whose weakest link defines its success potential. The managerial approach used in HLS must consider all these factors and more to be effective.

Now it is time to consider the contribution of intelligence in the HLS setting.

HLS and Intelligence

Knowledge is power, its application an art.

HLS is about dissuasion, detection, and prevention of malicious acts. Until now, we've focused mainly on the creation of security strategies, the supporting organizations and infrastructures, and the human factor, including that all-important first line of engagement: the detection-and-prevention line manned by security agents. But we should, momentarily, touch on intelligence. While the information given below is known and obvious to many, it is added here for the sake of completeness and will be kept as brief as possible.

Obviously, we do not want to be taken by surprise when it comes to HLS planning, strategies, and decisions that impact our prevention success-probability. Wherever and whenever possible we would like to have at least preliminary information about perpetrators, their plans, targets, and means. In the same way businesses collects information about competitors to better devise plans and strategies, HLS too is, or should be, in the business of information gathering, at least to some extent.

This chapter will discuss the advantages of having such preliminary information, though we will not discuss the means, sources, and other relevant information. We will, for the time being, accept intelligence as a black box that provides us with advance information about potential threats. This black box may include any type or combination of intelligence sources, depending on the assets to be protected, their value, importance, and public profile.

Intelligence can also become a double-edged sword when experts carefully manipulate it to deceive the enemy. As intelligence is not the subject matter of this book, and for the sake of simplicity, we will assume intelligence received is reasonably reliable.

The Use of Intelligence

What intelligence provides is the opportunity to increase the probability of a security organization preventing perpetrators from achieving their malicious goals. This is simple common sense–the more one knows, the more one can appropriately prepare for possible events, increasing dissuasion, detection, and prevention probability. As stated earlier: *forewarned is forearmed*.

Let us assume, as an example, that information arrived pointing at a potential malicious threat advancing toward a border. This information might include a general description of the number of people involved, the load being carried by a vehicle, or weapons being used. Once this information is received and processed, an attempt to stop this threat can be put into motion leveraging local, regional, and state forces. In this case, our last line of defense would be the border control point–official or not. But what we have achieved is advanced warning, which gives us more time to alert, prepare, and put forces in motion. Border agents are alert to what is coming, and perhaps we have even given them an opportunity to intercept the threat before it reaches that last line of defense, further increasing prevention probability. Like driving a car on a straight road, visibility is now excellent and the driver can assess if other drivers are in control of their vehicles and driving safely, as opposed to driving on mountainous, curving roads where visibility is bad and warning of potential hazards is smaller. The need for intelligence is further amplified when multiple events are concerned, where some events might be distractions, where force-dilution considerations are involved, and in other cases requiring clear decisions on how, where, when, and in what scale to react.

In security, we refer to "security circles," circles that fan outward around the protected asset(s). Each such circle must first detect and then delay perpetrators to increase the available reaction time for the next inner circle to prepare and react. Many of these circles include physical elements such as fences, doors, CCTV, or access controls. What intelligence provides us with is an additional virtual-detection circle, one whose distance from the protected asset can be thousands of miles, one whose contour keeps changing. The earlier and further away detection takes place, the longer security has to prepare itself and therefore prevent or contain an event.

The converse of this, of course, is lack of intelligence, which may come from mistaken analysis or interpretation, or an inability to act upon said intelligence, resulting in surprises and negative outcomes. This happens all the time: in pre-war, warfare, crime and terrorism; in medicine, industry, and research. Obviously, lack of intelligence is something to be avoided as much as possible, leading to the question: should defensive security organizations, those who are the last line of defense, deal with intelligence gathering or just be users thereof? The author of this book thinks that defensive security forces should not be the intelligence gatherers, for the following reasons:

- HLS has a defensive role. It is not an intelligence agency; it is not for HLS to collect intelligence or to analyze or interpret it. HLS must rely on other organizations to provide operational intelligence after it has been processed by the respective agency, after the quality of sources is assessed, and after information is analyzed and interpreted.

- HLS is the last line of defense for nationwide security, both physical and cyber. HLS should focus on last-line detection and prevention, on preparedness and alertness, on its core competence;

- Finally, it is far better to have a false alarm than a surprise event, or "better safe than sorry," meaning that HLS should consider *all* intelligence that comes into its hands and react upon it, not interpret and analyze it, which may be prone to human biases.

The use of intelligence is not obvious, but it is easier when the wider picture and context of the different types of threats are understood as done by dedicated intelligence agencies. The arguments for the use of and importance of intelligence are obvious, but what does this entail in practice?

Intelligence in Practice

Security chiefs and their organizations should collect intelligence from all accessible sources using whatever means are available to them, including police forces reporting on crimes, national security agencies and terror reports, the military, and others. The intelligence that is collected is sorted into several types, but the part that interests HLS organizations is operational security, meaning intelligence that can be acted and reacted upon to trick and stop an opponent. Once operational intelligence has been received, the types of actions depend upon the protected assets in question, locations, priorities, and available means.

HLS operational intelligence can be divided into two key types: event intelligence and perpetrator intelligence. Understanding a perpetrator's culture, motivations, and nuances (language, slang, or body language) is essential when looking at event-specific intelligence and visualizing perpetrators. This non-event-specific information is used throughout to analyze and understand potential contexts like a hostage situation, potential behavior (will they negotiate and how hard), or reactions (will they kill hostages). Such knowledge and understanding developed by intelligence analysts helps prepare field agents to identify patterns and coded language, to profile people, and to recognize suspicious elements. Agents and officers should know, for example, the level of perpetrator determination. Is she or he willing to commit suicide? Are they loners or part of an organization?

People profiling is an art, one that is necessary for security agents to master. On-site profiling is a last-line, operational-intelligence-collection opportunity to identify suspects and perpetrators and prevent their malicious actions.

Event-specific information is operational, calling for a proactive response within said understanding of the perpetrators, assets, risks, etc. involved. Operational intelligence must be moved into the field as quickly as possible. Procrastination results in failed prevention, shorter alert and preparation times, and too-short reaction times.

Add up intelligence received on events and perpetrators to on-site profiling, and we have a large part of our tactical intelligence black box, the information needed to help security agents be as forewarned as possible.

But how should this intelligence then be used? Leadership and staff need to exercise their thinking, expand their knowledge, counter their conclusions, brainstorm, and attempt to come up with the most sensible operational conclusions. When in doubt, more frequent assessment should be done considering local and global developments. When this goes wrong, disaster can ensue. In a previous chapter, we mentioned the case of Arabic messages concerning 9/11 not translated until after the fact, due to lack of (post-fact) correct prioritization. Information is key; information can save lives. Intelligence must be prioritized, analyzed, and shared, or we risk what may become devastating consequences.

In turn, HLS agents must be able to respond appropriately to received intelligence, not falling into the trap of thinking only along protocol lines. Agents should, to use a platitude, "think outside of the box," identify weak points, and decide on the effective use of forces and resources.

The overall cycle is delicate because of the human touch on which it is based, and because of biases, dilution, and shifts in understanding that occur from the receipt of raw intelligence until it is converted into specific operational HLS activities. Reducing the drift of preconceived ideas involves listening to "devil's advocates"–those with different belief systems, people who identify dissonances, who are independent thinkers able to offer different conclusions within the context. Hierarchical thinking must be avoided; the situation where only the top, say, five chiefs can think and the rest of the team must execute is risky, calling for strengthened knowledge and thinking independence for field and other agents.

In addition to the above, intelligence inputs from field

agents must not be underestimated; field agents see people, behaviors, patterns, and abnormalities that can be or construe intelligence. Proactive, thinking leadership will encourage and exploit this ability to gather additional information, experiences, and insights from field agents to expose and develop additional intelligence-related considerations. This information is integrated into the big picture, improving understanding of strengths and weaknesses and extraction of operational conclusions.

In practice, this is all challenging. Not least because of operational pressures, the time factor, available resources, and other practical limitations. But as difficult as it may be, HLS should receive information but also provide it backward to improve cooperation and understanding and to better refine security.

The Human Factor

Toward the end of the 20th century, US government decided to reduce human intelligence (HUMINT) and increase electronic intelligence-gathering. HUMINT is slow, local, and more than once found to be unreliable when agents and spies crossed the lines. Electronic interception like ECHELON, which is said to intercept millions of messages an hour, is much more efficient. But that efficiency isn't always for the better because these messages need to be analyzed, put in context, prioritized, and disseminated. The latter actions are led or done by humans–analysts or programmers–so that in practice the bottleneck has been shifted from field agents to office analysts.

Field agents, able to assess the reliability of sources and cross-check information, can alert the back office of the importance, reliability and urgency of certain information and, get it to the "top of the pile" for immediate attention. Good officers and analysts, despite being overburdened with threats and information, do a great job in sorting and prioritizing information. This can be done much more successfully when information is concentrated and shared, because single pieces of information might be meaningless or receive low priority while many little pieces put together create a coherent, maybe alarming conclusion.

Therefore, it is for the better to combine first-hand human sources in the field to verify and cross-check information. This provides stronger conclusions than those generated by a single agency using only, for example, intercepted data and voice.

Technology is there to support, not replace, humans. What technology really does is shift the bottleneck from one person to another, from one type of expertise to a different one. To create intelligence, sources of information must be expanded and diversified, egos put aside, allowing brainstorming and teamwork. Gathered information and Intelligence staff must represent a variety of perspectives including that of field agents. This need for HUMINT has been raised again following the 9/11 tragic events.

Whether we're talking intelligence, decision making, operation, or any other facet of HLS, there is one potential problem that must always be kept at the forefront, and that's what I like to call "simplification sins," which is where we next turn.

Simplification Sins

*"Politics is the art of looking for trouble, finding
it everywhere, diagnosing it incorrectly, and
applying the wrong remedies." – Groucho Marx*

Throughout our lives, we humans tend to choose the easy,
paved way to simplify our lives. In doing this we respond
to whims, social pressures, authority, knowledge, experience,
forces, and behaviors that bias our lives. This is true whether
we're speaking of our personal lives, families, friends, social
events, communities, or professional lives. We buy brands because our friends do, or adopt behaviors that superiors or role
models exhibit. In a sense, we give up a part of our personality
and will (consciously or not) to fit in or be included. We also
make decisions that we feel will simplify our lives, but end
up not doing so, generally because we find out our decisions
were flawed, our gut instincts wrong, or maybe because we're
following orders, rules, or societal constructs that we do not
properly understand, need, or identify with. So, we align ourselves and follow standards our environment sets; we simplify

to avoid intellectual challenges; we simplify because we go for the lowest-hanging fruit. These and other simplification sins are the ones that dilute, reduce, or drift strategy, planning, and execution from the original vision, which itself is also affected by biases of the one(s) conceiving it.

What is important is that this happens not only with our behaviors but also with our thought processes–in which emotions, state of mind, egos, fears, prior experience, our ability to see details or the big picture, our patience, and many others that can be summarized as gut feelings bias our decisions. Decisions may be about anything, from choosing a perfume to identifying threats, deciding on strategies, assessing risks, evaluating personnel, choosing equipment, studying a subject, making a design, or writing procedures. Mostly unaware, we use these biases to help simplify our lives and stick to comfort zones.

While we can't eliminate these biases, awareness of them and of the tendency toward simplification in general helps us neutralize them, improving our decision making and leading to better choices. This chapter discusses some examples and aspects of simplification and biases, no matter if we are a leader or a simple agent.

Delegation of Incompetence

The delegation of authority and responsibility is a known practice; however, this is not the only type of delegation. There is a flip side: the aware or unaware delegation of incompetence. In this context, incompetence refers to the gap between responsibilities and abilities, between authority and the motivation to properly exercise it, and between required and actual know-how.

Such delegation is counterproductive all the way to being dangerous, often touched by ego, fear, paralysis, or naivety. Behind it are many reasons: not wanting to admit inability, fear of failure, fear from superiors, laziness, indecision, or perhaps just politics. Many managers and employees tend to get rid of "hot potatoes" by delegating them under sophisticated pretexts and then expecting others to either do the work for them or to steer the delegator toward a decision, hopefully the right one. In short, delegators of incompetence seek to simplify matters for themselves by delegating responsibility to someone else, irrespective of the consequences. We also delegate incompetence to technology, contractors, consultants, family, peers, and superiors—in short, all over.

Delegation of incompetence supposedly makes our lives easier in the short term, but it always floats in the long term. Let us look at some examples:

- Development of security plans requires a lot of thought, but many planners prefer to copy existing plans and adjust them to the project at hand. The fact that the spirit and logic of the existing plan biases the new plan is overlooked, leaving points uncovered or others overprotected.

- Is it right to rely only on technology to detect threats? No. As discussed, technology has very specific detection performance; it can alarm on, say, metals carried by people. It cannot profile people, alarm on abnormal human behavior, or integrate information from other sources. Technology mirrors the ingenuity of its designers within the constraints of physics, chemistry and engineering; it does necessarily cover all threats within its technical domain.

- One high-ranking police commander told me in a conversation that his decisions are driven by the next board of inquiry. Over-legalization and post-factum inquiries shifted his attention from doing what was right to doing what was safe for him and his job. It's easy to criticize after the fact than make good decisions beforehand, thus freezing daring, creativity, and initiative.

- "I followed procedures" is a very typical answer given after something went wrong. It implies "I am not to blame–it is the procedures," thus delegating our lack of creativity, initiative, and daring under very specific circumstances to generic paperwork and those who wrote it.

- Planning activities relying only on intelligence is also risky. We cannot justify such reliance alone unless we expand the breadth and scope of our planning to include a perpetrator's profile, thinking, and daring. Such understanding can help assess perpetrator's creativity and last-minute maneuvers, for example. This is especially true when small criminal or terror groups are involved, who for a variety of reasons make last-minute changes in their plans. We cannot delegate our lack of imagination to the fact that we had certain intelligence at a specific point in time. Think of the intelligence that drove the 2003–2011 Iraq war.

- We sometimes over-explain ourselves to the point of creating misunderstandings, simply because we are unable to formulate ideas into simple words and short sentences. We delegate our inability to clearly formulate ideas, expecting listeners to separate chaff from grain.

There is a fine line between following rules because they make sense and suit the occasion, and following rules blindly to the point of oblivion. "Rules are for the obedience of fools and the guidance of wise men" is a famous quote attributed to World War II RAF ace pilot Sir Douglas Bader. Delegation of incompetence is all over. From field agents to top decision makers, no one is free of it.

Where the Means Become the Goal

Not only in the world of HLS, but in all areas, people become so enmeshed with following protocol that they miss the big picture and forget why they and the protocol are in place to begin with. I once flew into Mexico City, connecting through

Atlanta. On my way there, my 91-ounce, mostly empty after-shave bottle went through security without a problem; on the way back, it was confiscated. The security agent was negligent or chose to let me through, overlooking the rule stating that up to 90-ounce bottles are allowed. Upon my return, the security agent spotted the aftershave bottle, opened my bag, saw it was 91 ounces, and became stubborn. I involved her superior, who because of rules insisted that the mostly empty bottle be confiscated. That one extra ounce printed on the bottle, but certainly missing in it, made all the difference. There was no room for on-the-spot decision making, no flexibility, no independent thought, only the rule. Moreover, their adamant behavior made it clear to me that they failed in their real mission: to detect and stop threats. Their mission suddenly became to blindly follow procedures. It was a sad realization.

Another example was related to me by an airline security chief who, upon visiting one US airport, saw police officers entering the passenger-only area. The security agent asked them to take off their service belts and badge and pass them through the X-ray machine. The belts were loaded with their guns, bullets, and handcuffs. The chief asked the TSA agent what exactly she was looking for inspecting the belts in the X-ray machine. She replied: "I am just following orders." The police officers were clearly carrying guns and could shoot passengers at will or in a psychotic rampage. If the "system" trusts the officers, let them through; if not, then take away their guns or fire them altogether. Moreover, it makes no sense to screen

102

their belts and badges if an emergency is taking place.

Following rules and procedures discourages and debilitates the intellect of managers, employees, supervisors, and agents to the point where they lose judgment altogether. Such loss of judgment obviously continues in an emergency, affecting their response precisely when it is most needed. There is no split personality in which in routine we are followers and in emergencies we become leaders.

The Dalai Lama XIV suggests: "Know the rules well, so you can break them effectively" while the artist Pablo Picasso recommends that you "learn the rules like a pro, so you can break them like an artist." Simply said–there is not a single man-made rule in the world that fits all situations, people, and locations. The void between reality and rules is filled by people's intellect, just like judges do when applying laws to specific legal cases. Neutralizing intellect and daring perpetuates the void and leaves the secured exposed.

One rare and courageous example that must be mentioned here is that of the four leaders who took the initiative and acted against the hijackers of United Airlines Flight 93 en route from Newark to San Francisco on September 11, 2001. The hijackers planned to crash the plane in Washington DC, but Mark Bingham, Todd Beamer, Thomas Burnett, and Jeremy Glick decided to act and carried out their plan. Their judgment and reflexes told them what needed to be done, and they did it. They were not concerned with keeping protocol, from turning on cell phones and moving around the cabin all the way to deciding the fate of fellow humans. Each of them, in his own way, was trained to expect the unexpected and dare to react. They understood that death is imminent and at least tried to reverse their fate.

Hurricane Katrina exposed the ineffectiveness of the Department of Homeland Security and its Federal Emergency Management Agency (FEMA), which apparently had all the means to reduce loss of life and property. A series of indecisions and lack of leadership led to overlooking the need to prepare for such sorrowful days. The head of the DHS ignored the storm, saying he relied on the FEMA director to prepare, who in turn blamed state and local officials in Louisiana and the media for the post-storm slow response. The public later learned that FEMA's head was not qualified to fulfill his position. The head of FEMA was a political appointee, rather than a professional one, who not only lacked the background and experience to fulfill his role but seems to have also lacked motivation to do so. Preparations would not stop the storm but could have reduced the loss of lives and accelerated overall recovery efforts. Everybody blamed (delegated their incompetence), but no one accepted responsibility.

Yes, HLS rules and procedures are in place for a reason, and that reason is to protect the public and provide defensive security and recovery operations. The reason is not rules, structure, or discipline; these are means. HLS systems–such as the TSA, immigration, and customs–are so massive that performance and discipline must be practiced to achieve uniformity

104

across the system; but in many cases, the rigidity with which it is done turns the means into an end. It causes end-of-the-line agents to focus on procedures and appeasing bosses rather than on detecting real threats, illegal immigrants, or contraband. After all, it is the boss who determines promotions, not the customer or the probability of a real security event.

From a different perspective, overstressing procedures and relinquishing freedom of initiative and thought kills the "soul," the reason for which the means are there to begin with. When that goal is lost, the purpose, focus, and respective sensitivities are lost along with it. Instead of practicing security, we practice procedures; instead of developing sensitivities to behaviors, we focus on operating machines and the formalities of identification. The soul of the procedures and rules is their essence, which includes the extra, intangible detection of human vibes that makes the difference, such as looking the passenger in the eye when comparing IDs with boarding passes. Our focus can become so lost that at times, the "system" chooses to ignore non-conformal signs, resulting in prevention failure, such as the Fort Hood case in which a military psychiatrist shot dead several soldiers inside the base.

How does this fit into our theme of the delegation of incompetence? When we give up our own judgment, will, and daring and, commit ourselves to procedures instead, we latently delegate our incompetence. And as for the greater theme of simplification, is it not easier to simply follow the rules than to think, decide, and act for oneself?

Technology's Effect on People

We will deal with technology in depth in the next chapter, but it would be remiss not to mention it briefly here. The use of, over-reliance on, and misunderstandings surrounding technology used in the security field are all simplification errors. They fall under the heading of delegation of incompetence because in some (if not many) cases, humans delegate their abilities, judgment, or senses to a machine. This can obviously lead to mistakes and inefficiency, as we will cover in a later chapter.

One case of such incompetence is the following:

A cellular telephone company reached its maturity stage and hired McKinsey & Co. to reduce costs and shrink staff. One of the cost centers marked by McKinsey as requiring cost reduction was security. Initially, a 200-person security consulting company was hired to develop the new security concept and show its cost benefits. The company's key recommendations were that no cost reduction was possible, but that certain equipment should be replaced with newer versions. Eventually, the client reached out to us; we did the study and presented alternative solutions all the way down to return on investment. After gaining his personal trust, the executive in charge, a man in his 50's, commented on the first company's work that: "This is the first time in my career that I totally rejected a consultant's recommendations." The original report presented by our competition reflected the consultants' incompetence: their inability to solve their client's problem, inability to think creatively and, the consultants' fall into the technology trap. Clearly people, risk, and mitigation skills were missing.

Use of Consultants

As a final example of the delegation of incompetence, let us look at the use of consultants.

To properly use consultants, managers need to identify specific needs and then assign consultants to bridge specific knowledge, ability, or time gaps. Such gaps could be shortage of manpower or lack of specific knowledge, abilities, technological expertise, or other. When hiring consultants, one needs to be clear as to what he or she expects from the consultant and to eventually assess his deliverables. Consultants are not to be confused with mentors, and they should not be used to "cover our backs" with an "expert opinion of a third, independent party."

Many decision makers make poor or unjustified use of their consultants when they unknowingly expect them to fulfill executive roles such as providing leadership or make critical or essential decisions for which management is responsible. In other instances, managers do not sanity-check consultants' recommendations. Let us look at a few examples.

A wealthy Mexican family hires a security consultant to improve the family's security. Among the recommendations is the use of armored cars. The family buys such cars without understanding that an armored car alone is not enough; one must consider not only the access to and from the car when entering and exiting it but also what happens in case of an attack or accident, which may trap the passengers inside the car and prolong rescue operations. The consultant, in an attempt to reduce scope and costs, limited his recommendation to protection, overlooking contingency responses and consequences, focusing his effort on the high-value goods (cars) and not the human soft skills.

The management of a company offering industrial real estate and logistics parks hired a security consultant to improve park security. Aiming to impress, the consultant proposed a variety of electronic systems and a control center. He overlooked the fact that guards were not properly screened and that the fence perimeter had several breaches. Clearly, management trusted the well-paid consultant without making any sanity checks or questioning the conclusions.

Let us look at a business example: The leadership of a well-known US corporation decided to reduce corporate costs. Targeting 20% savings, the corporation hired one of the top consulting firms to analyze the company, find where cost reductions could be made, and come up with an implementable action plan. The consulting firm sent in a group of young analysts to study the organization and collect data and information. Upon seeing the initial data, and rightfully assuming that client executives would oppose the recommended cuts, the lead consultants instead recommended an increased cost-reduction goal, assuming that this would eventually be negotiated down to the required 20%. Months went by before the study and planning were concluded, during which decisions about new and existing activities went into limbo. When management did receive the report, they implemented the recommendations per *their* understanding of the report and its spirit.

The result of all this was loss of time and money because of the limbo period, implementation time, loss of profits, and increased costs that eventually failed to achieve the targeted savings. Why such a poor result? Because of loss of corporate momentum, employee slowdowns, deflection of focus, and biased implementation of the recommendations. All of this could have been avoided had management instead exercised *their responsibility*, rolled up their sleeves, done the study, and made decisions. After all, they should know their organization far better that anyone else.

The problem was that the corporation's top management delegated its own incompetence to the consulting firm and then implemented the firm's recommendations. Top management–who should have best known corporate activities, priorities, markets, and other considerations–should have led the cost-cutting analysis and implementation themselves, not delegated the task out. Moreover, this should have and could have been done without deflecting the corporation's focus from its real goals to serving the consultants and their need for information.

Failure in such cases is inevitable for several reasons:

- Consultants are not bound or expected to know the security issues better than management does;

- Consultants write reports and propose actions based on

their understanding of the issues at hand and *their* filters like education, and experience, which may be very different from the client's;

- In turn, management and staff implement consultants' recommendations through *their* filters which normally are different from the consultants';

- The process itself is time consuming, putting activities on hold and negatively affecting results;

- Consultants make their recommendations and leave, but management remains with the responsibility and any mistakes introduced;

- The use of consultants incurs costs, when the aim was to cut costs. These costs include:

  · Direct consultant costs;

  · Employee time and lack of professional focus during consultant interviews;

  · The time it takes management and employees to read and implement consultant recommendations;

  · Errors and gaps between consultant theory and implementation practice, and resulting misunderstandings or misinterpretations. In addition, changes in the security environment between the time data was collected and the time implementation is completed also affect results.

And we can take this even further, since:

- Consultants also make mistakes;

- When consultants become lead figures in a task, management tends to drop its guard, thereby reducing controls and sanity checks;

- In any case, management will be held responsible for consultants' mistakes, making it more logical for management to make its own.

While it might seem simpler to hire a consulting company–a time saver, even–there is no real alternative to good management. A consultant-led general planning rarely succeeds as planned because consultants do not know the intangibles, the people, the spirit, culture, critical details, or trade secrets that all converge into making a security organization–or a company, for that matter. Think of a non-expert doctor performing surgery following a consultant's advice. Would it work? Probably not. The use of consultants should be under a clear understanding of mutual expectations, tasks to be fulfilled, and deliverables, otherwise it boils down to delegation of incompetence.

Many consultants, advisors, experts, lobbyists, and other narrow-interest functionaries hover over the HLS world, making their living off it. Few of them are accountable for the outcome of their work. Some focus on the big picture, overlooking details, while others are detail oriented. The challenge is to have those who connect crucial details with the big picture. At the end of the day, it is up to leadership to rely on its people to devise flexible, adaptable, dynamic, responsive, and effective HLS organizations supported by respective intelligence, technology, and procedures.

Human Biases

Human biases form part of the previously discussed Human Factor. They are the qualitative, immeasurable, unquantifiable ingredient we humans bring into our lives like fear, ego, love, and hate. In most cases, we are unaware that we are biased or we prefer to deny it. Think of moods, ability to withstand pressures, our happiness, economic aspects, and other parameters that integrate into a gut feeling affecting our biases. We all feel free to delegate decisive drivers of our decision making to our biases and gut feelings which affect our preferences, choices and doubts.

Human biases are all over, affecting each one of us, from presidents and congressmen to security leaders, commanders, and field agents. They affect our qualitative-based decisions like policy decisions, our trust in people and their abilities, our choices of technology, scope of procedures, and the way we treat subordinates or bend over with superiors. Awareness to and of such biases helps us judge if these are constructive or destructive. Do these strengthen or weaken our standing vis-à-vis the subject matter, its long-term impact, human lives, knowledge and asset protection, or costs? Let us look at some examples.

A year and a half after the 1973 war initiated by Egypt and

Syria against Israel, CIA Deputy Director General Vernon Walters said in a lecture to the US Army Security Agency Training Center and School[19]: "We had a report in CIA in late May 1973 that said, 'Egypt and Syria will start war against Israel on the 6th of October'." "We duly reported this," Walters continued. "But one of my experiences with the intelligence business has been that the analysts generally shrink from telling you something unpleasant, and even after we try to fit every piece of intelligence in to show that it wasn't going to happen on the 6th of October. We finally got ourselves convinced that it wasn't going to happen on the 6th of October. As a matter of fact, I'm the guy that signed the Watch Report that said it wasn't going to happen that Saturday morning, and it happened that Saturday afternoon." In other words, managements prefer to buy positive news, not spend money on bad ones.[20]

Another example is the way intelligence was used to drive the 2003–2011 Iraq War. Both President Bush and Vice President Cheney wished to overthrow Saddam Hussein, but to justify these actions in a post-9/11 world, they needed a moral reason. That reason was found in the suspicion that Saddam Hussein was developing chemical and nuclear weapons, weapons of mass destruction (WMD). In other words, a goal was already marked; all else was arranged simply to justify that goal. Human bias, in the form of the government's desire to overthrow

---

[19] http://www.haaretz.com/israel-news/.premium-1.747188

[20] https://www.amazon.com/Business-Decisions-Success-Intuition-Accelerate/dp/9657569028/ref=tmm_pap_swatch_0?_encoding=UTF8&qid=&sr=

a foreign leader, was responsible for making a qualitative set of decisions. The outcome of these decisions is not necessarily right or wrong–that is not the point. The point is that the process used to come to these decisions was biased by the desire to achieve a certain goal. After the fact, failed intelligence was blamed for the inability to find WMD. Decision makers delegated their incompetence to intelligence agencies–a rather unfair approach considering that finding such weapons was only a justification for the invasion.

The tool of awareness to such intangibles is important, sometimes critical, like the case of the 1986 attempted bombing of an ELAL airliner flying from London to Tel Aviv, Israel. In 1984, Anne-Marie Murphy, an Irish woman working in London, met Nezar Hindawi, a Jordanian who had immigrated to the UK and became her fiancé. When Murphy was five months pregnant, Hindawi convinced her to visit Israel and get married there in the presence of his parents, sending her off on the ELAL flight to Tel Aviv, explaining that for various reasons he would arrive later. He generously paid for her new passport, clothing, and suitcase and took her to Heathrow Airport on April 17, 1986, instructing her not to tell Israeli security personnel that she was engaged to an Arab. Murphy was unaware that Hindawi's generosity was for a reason–the suitcase had a false bottom containing over a kilogram of Semtex, an explosive that X-ray machines cannot detect. After passing all security points, Murphy reached the pre-boarding Israeli security agents, who did their routine questioning. Murphy was cool, lied as instructed, but wasn't aware of the bomb that was to kill her a few hours after takeoff. Something didn't fit in her story and, as questioning went on, in her behavior as well. Thus, the Israeli agent decided to thoroughly check her suitcase, which, after being emptied, was suspiciously heavy, leading to the discovery of the explosive and trigger device. Murphy was as surprised as the security agents, whose people-oriented approach, questioning, and human sensitivity saved Murphy's life and those of almost 400 additional passengers and crew members. Hindawi was detained before boarding a later flight to Damascus, where he would continue plotting the next mass-murder action for the Syrian Air Force intelligence. Here, an alert agent identified a threat where routine security checks failed.

On December 21, 1988, Pan Am Flight 103 (Frankfurt to Detroit via London and New York) exploded over Scotland and crashed partially into a Lockerbie (Scotland) residential area, killing 270 passengers, crew, and Lockerbie residents. Investigation–also based on anonymous phone calls to the American embassy in Helsinki, Finland–suggests that an innocent passenger checked in the explosive suitcase, not knowing the fate she or he faced. In this case, pre-boarding security agents and methodologies failed to identify either suspicious passenger stories or behaviors.

The ELAL airliner was saved by the combination of a good procedure, training, and the security agent's qualitative judgment of the person and her story. The agent and his gut feelings were the last line of defense to which Anne-Marie Murphy and many others owe their life. The security agent's awareness to his gut feelings, which biased his judgment and subsequent decision to empty the suitcase, was critical. In the Lockerbie case, routine security checks were relied upon and failed, as did security agents, possibly through no fault of their own (due perhaps to inadequate training, personal circumstances, or any one of several factors that can cause the "human" link in the security chain to break).

Biases in General

Some biases are presented below. These may be latent, apparent, aware or unaware, explicit or implicit, or reveal themselves in a variety of forms and opportunities. The following table exemplifies sample relationships between adjectives describing biases and their potential impact on security outcomes. For example, a tired security agent will not be alert, and focused agents will not be distracted.

The list can be expanded to include personality and behavioral descriptions like ego, impatience, generalization, simplification, personal communications, perception, suspicious, comfort zones, negative/positive thinking, compromise, yielding, curiosity, culture, and others. Each of these alone and any combination thereof affect the quality and consistency of our judgment and reactions.

Let us briefly look at some real-life examples: A normally lenient judge becomes merciless the day after his son's mo-

Adjective	Security Opportunity or Risk
Courage	Ability to face challenging situations
Integrity	Honest and professional work
Focus, concentration	Not to be distracted from the task at hand: preventive security
Fear, timid	Inability to face aggressive passengers or contain challenging situations
Greed	Risk of bribe
Over-imaginative	Wrong interpretation of events, poor memory recollection
Omission	Giving up or missing elements that may prove critical

torcycle is stolen. An off-duty police officer is tense from a day's work, detains a driver whom he thinks isn't cautious enough, and unloads his frustration on the driver. A neurosurgeon suffering from advanced liver cancer refuses to give up his beloved profession, fails to disclose his situation, and continues to perform head operations, resulting in the need of repeat surgery. Awareness and integrity could have saved all these and others much inconvenience.

Sensitivity to and detection of human behaviors is based on

human training, abilities, and personal judgment, which create a wide range of additional risk-detection opportunities.

Additional Bias Examples

Some general human bias examples and their effect are shared herein. These are generally valid in environments in which people interact, including security environments:

- Emotions that result in reactions rather than cold-headed, proactive actions;

- Egos not admitting mistakes, which then grow to mass proportions;

- Fear to dare; fear of strong and talented subordinates; fear of responsibility;

- Communications and misunderstandings;

- Gut feelings telling me "this is right;"

- Omissions by choice or unawareness;

- Simplification and minimization by choice or unawareness;

- Choices between alternatives: we limit alternatives to begin with; we choose wrong alternatives; we choose the simplest or lesser-effort alternative;

- Compromise and lack of leadership;

- Unwarranted reliance on third parties;

- Ongoing refinancing of debt instead of debt reduction. Typical to over-leveraged companies and households;

- Personal and group drive: willingness to tackle a challenge vs. sticking to comfort zones;

- Integrity and courage to admit failure;

- Two people see the same event but recount it differently and have different understanding of it;

- Cultural misunderstandings;

Let us look at a few cases of independent analysis and judgment (or misjudgment) of situations or information:

- Years ago, a technician went to visit a security center in which a new standby power backup system was installed. He met the person in charge, who bloomed with compliments about the system and its reliability. The technician decided to go see the system, finding out that it was switched off. Luckily for the security company and the system supplier, there were no power outages, so this minor but critical human oversight was not exposed during a crisis.

- One day in August 2008, I coincidentally heard Dr. Ben Bernanke announcing his first monetary expansion targeting US Banks. I am not a great economist, but my understanding is that banks are not supposed to need emergency cash unless there is a problem. Against the advice of my brokers, I sold off most of my traded stocks. In

October, when the collapse began, my broker had a different view of my actions.

- Smart failure is like making Granny's beloved soup, which we seek to imitate and yet is never quite right. We use all the correct ingredients, pot, cooking time, and still, it is different. We probably miss the spice of love. Security is quite similar in that we do everything "right" and yet there are failures, including the examples recounted in this book.

- Cultural and origin biases are another aspect in which biases play a major role. We tend to automatically be more alert and suspicious of people originating from certain parts of the world or people with different-colored skin from us. Agents educated in the West will be less sensitive to the facial expressions of people from Southeast Asia, where emotions are not as expressive, and will be more suspicious of people with certain looks or accents.

The Trap of Capital Investments

According to TSA statistics, no real terror threats have been prevented[21] in US airports. Yes, weapons, drugs, aftershave bottles, and other elements were confiscated, but how many of their holders were real perpetrators? How many led to the exposure of terror cells? How many of the confiscated ele-

---

[21] http://blog.tsa.gov/2014/01/tsa-blog-year-in-review-2013.html
http://www.slate.com/articles/news_and_politics/explainer/2010/11/
does_the_tsa_ever_catch_terrorists.html

ments were transported with no violent motivation vs. how many were meant to cause damage? The flip side is also of interest, but the answer is unknown: How many guns and other prohibited elements were *not* detected despite going through screening? Capital investments, a big part of which is in technology, do not necessarily improve security as seen when in 2015 the TSA failed 95% of airport-security tests conducted by the Department of Homeland Security inspector general's office. Was it the people? The equipment? Procedures? Or maybe the overall concept.

Money gives a sense of power, and the higher the budgets, the more powerful one feels. The "big money" is in equipment, thus catching industry, lobbyists', and decision makers' attention, in many cases causing a shift in priorities and judgment as discussed below.

The first driver is a mistaken assumption that technology in general has the power to compensate for human gaps in ability and performance, as discussed in the next chapter. Technology can also deflect security agents' attention from security to operating detection machines, both being obvious mistakes.

Yet big money always draws interested parties, pressing decision makers into choosing their solution, be it the solution in principle or their specific equipment. This then becomes a major focus-consumer of the decision maker, who in many cases finds her- or himself neglecting concepts, the way a specific technology fits into the big picture, and security related intangibles that define success. But still, many decision makers are trapped in the shiny-equipment performance, compromising on performance or buying practically useless equipment altogether.

On top of external pressures, there is a little ego tickling us from within. As people, we want to pride ourselves in signing billion-dollar contracts; it is far less glamorous to sign off billion-dollar payrolls and training budgets. The result is not always success or even partial success; it is minimization (of the HLS idea) caused by sensation. It is not easy to stand up and oppose priorities set by a group of interested people, nor is it easy to pull everyone "above the water" to see and accept the big picture and the minor role the equipment has there. Discussed in the next chapter, SBInet is one case where this has happened.

Another aspect that should impact capital investments is that of perpetrator dynamics: block them in one place, and they will find a way around. Block them in main airports, and they will target smaller ones; secure passenger boarding, and they will move to cargo; block cargo, and they will move to delivery. Thus, high-capital investments serve to shift perpetrators from one crack in the rock to another, from one creative solution to the next, creating an unending need for new investments.

As previously discussed, perpetrators are faster moving than large HLS organizations. One creative success made by perpetrators in circumventing detection may deem a whole equipment investment useless.

The flip side is capital savings, as exemplified by the following case: In mid-2016, I was invited by one of the world-leading industrial and logistic park companies to review the security of one of their Latin American parks located in a high-risk zone. We visited the park and its surroundings, talked to people, and collected relevant information later analyzed and converted into an action plan. The work also included risks, priorities and practical recommendations on how to increase park security. Robbery–including armed, of trucks loaded with pharmaceuticals or consumer electronics of brands operating in the park–was identified as the top risk. The client chose not to invest in improving security until six months later that armed robbery occurred and overspending took place.

As with many such security studies, nothing was done with the recommendations because of budget, profit, and return-on-investment issues. For such parks, security is a selling point to convince tenants to rent space in the park, but security is like the cleaning staff: (almost) transparent when there, well noticed when absent. This important point reflects our comfort zone, of wanting security but not being willing to pay for it or have it disrupt our daily lives. Clearly, this is true until terror or crime strikes close to us or our loved ones, turning experience into our teacher. The robbery was widely publicized, negatively impacting the park's image.

Capital investments are often a trap, mostly of comfort zones, sometimes of fantasy or shortsightedness. Here again, awareness of the pros and cons, technology life-expectancy, perpetrator creativity, and other big-picture factors help make better use of funds as long as external, biasing pressures are neutralized or we are at least aware of their impact.

Cultural Differences

It would be remiss to discuss simplification and biases without mentioning cultural differences, though the cultural question is addressed in other chapters of this book. Generally, we share an underlying assumption that potential perpetrators share the same education, upbringing, country, or regional culture as security organizations and their agents have. This underlying assumption has many drivers, one of them being that many of us simply do not know other cultures; we weren't exposed to them, nor have we interacted with them.

As an example of how culture affects understanding and respective decisions, let us look at body language. The body language of the Japanese differs from that of Italians, Koreans, or Americans. Differences also exist between regions and ethnicities, just like the differences between a Texan, a New Yorker, and a Californian. When attempting to profile potential perpetrators, a passenger's poker face could be mistaken for innocence, despite malicious intent being there. Japanese are careful to respect others' privacy by "minding their own business," not staring and scanning their subway environment. This may seem somewhat constrained to one who doesn't know the culture. Certain hand gestures understood by us to mean "one moment" or "you're kidding me" are understood as offensive by other cultures. Aggressive security-agent behavior or man-

124

ner of speech can stress innocent people not used to it.

On the other hand, it's safe to say that body language represents a very significant proportion of the messages conveyed and interpreted between people. Body-language experts agree that between 50% and 80% of all human communication is nonverbal. This implies that nonverbal communications are extremely important for understanding communications between people or lack thereof, particularly in face-to-face and one-on-one communications, and most definitely when those communications involve an emotional or attitudinal element.

Therefore, body language is important in security as well, but it needs to be understood within the cultural context. It is of great use when performing, for example, security screenings, questioning, or baggage searches, where the person's behavior can be far more revealing than any specific physical finding.

Culture also touches upon traditions and religion, like the use of the burqa, the face-hiding garment used by Muslim women that denies any face-identification possibility. Religious Muslim women are also averse to being touched for body searches. The Sikh tradition calls for men to wear traditional turbans covering their hair; religious people do not want to take them off in public, thus presenting an additional challenge to security screening. These and other such issues need to be identified and addressed by security methodologies.

Let me share with you such a cultural experience from my business life. As CEO of a company in which a major Japanese corporation has invested, I have experienced how cultural nuances can affect business. A $3-billion division of the Japanese corporation undertook to promote and sell our products in Japan, and, like every business, we had a champion or mentor who was the dealmaker on the Japanese side. At a certain point during our relationship, I sensed a change in our mentor's response speed to our emails; this turned into worry when email answers stopped altogether. I was worried because not answering emails is rude in Japanese culture, so something must have happened, but what? After two months, we received an email from our mentor apologizing for not answering the emails, informing us that he was leaving the company, and introducing his replacement.

We faced another uphill process to resell our company to the new mentor for him to drive sales and keep us high on his priority list. We welcomed the new mentor and offered all required assistance for him to study our product line and the business opportunity. As time went by, our new mentor, instead of updating us on his sales plans, politely delegated to us the job of putting together the business plan for sales in Japan as well as other activities. I also noted that he copied all his subordinates on the emails, skipping his superiors. I needed a response strategy, non-confrontational, polite, and positive. I decided to agree with all his requests, also asking him for his help with certain information needed to fulfill his requests. I made sure to copy his superiors as well as his subordinates on the emails. This was a test of patience, six months of useless and patient correspondence. Surprisingly, one day, the

Japanese gentleman called under instructions of his CEO asking for our permission to come and apologize in person for his behavior.

The new Japanese manager had different product-selling priorities in which we were not included. Thus, being non-confrontational as Japanese are, he avoided telling us the negative news, expecting us to let their commitments fade away. During his visit, we terminated our representation agreement, receiving a hefty compensation and gaining our freedom to reinitiate sales in the Japanese market.

When dealing with people, whether in business, security, or elsewhere, cultural differences must be considered and kept at the forefront. Overlooking or generalizing differences risks misunderstandings, miscommunications, and agents who cannot properly interpret evidence of malicious intent.

The Effect of Organization Size

Finally, we must mention the effect of organization size on decisions, simplifications, and biases. The smaller and friendlier an organization is, the faster it moves, and yet compromises tend to be made due to more personal friendships perhaps, or the closeness between employees and their superiors. We move quickly but may "cut corners" or skip protocols.

To ensure uniformity, big organizations are more rigid, less forgiving in terms of routine operations, and offer more career-promotion opportunities, which may shift staff attention from security to promotion and self-promotion campaigns.

This is especially true in governmental organizations where success and professionalism indexes – like time frames, budgets and deliverables – might be flexible. Large organizations tend to "protect their own", have coalitions and develop retaliation tactics against those who do not align with the majority; it is politics. Such partisan behaviors shift mental powers of some from security work to politics, lowering success probability of the entire HLS organization.

While organization size may not always be a controllable factor, it is important that we realize that organizations have their own biases and behaviors that influence how members of such an organization act and behave. In many cases, we see that the head figure, through his or her behavior, diffuses a certain spirit throughout the organization. If the head figure gossips, then gossip becomes the norm; if the head figure surrounds himself with weak yes-men, then the organization will be weak and lack constructive criticism; if the leader delegates, more is achieved.

In closing, let me repeat that the biases we hold and simplifications we resort to may not always be conscious, nor may they always be completely controlled. Yet knowing we are influenced by such factors can help us make more effective and less biased decisions. We need to proactively seek biases like "preparing for the last war" instead of future threats; what led me to choose a specific technology or how do I support and back my staff.

Technology has already been mentioned, both in this chapter and in preceding ones, and it's time now to look at the issue in more detail.

Technology

Do not defend what is known; research the unknown.

We have touched on technology several times in the preceding chapters, and now it is time to tackle HLS as a whole body. We are a technological society; nearly everything in our lives is touched by technology in some way, shape, or form–from the ways we entertain ourselves to how we stay healthy; from how we educate our children to the food we eat; from how we clean our dirty clothes to how we secure our homes, cars, and even country. The use of technology in the HLS setting is undoubtedly a necessity, but only when that technology is properly chosen, applied, and used. And even when used properly, technology is no substitute for well-trained personnel. There are two distinctly negative sides of technology that need to be discussed, and only by overcoming these can we effectively use technology in the HLS setting.

The Operational Perspective

The first of these perspectives involves technology from an operational standpoint, and as mentioned in the previous chapter, misunderstanding of technology leads to simplification errors of sorts. A big portion of our lives, abilities, and even emotions is delegated to technology. We delegate our memories to memory cards on smartphones, The Cloud or other means. Our feet are replaced by wheels. We don't handwrite letters anymore, thus missing another facet of personal communication. The internet knows it all, so we stop studying. And we consume mass produced fast food rather than cooking at home. But the comfort of automation doesn't come for free; it means that we depend on the reliability of equipment, on a continuous supply of electrical power, on programmers and hackers and our ability to work with or against them as appropriate, all of which brings the ultimate responsibility back to us humans. Though our standard of living rises, the quality of it generally degrades. This is also true for HLS.

Technology is used to replace or reduce dependency on the human factor. And while it is true that technology can work 24/7 and is more reliable in terms of failure rates, data acquisition, memory, processing, or output consistency, there are distinctly negative sides to relying on technology, to delegating our responsibilities to it, especially when we write off people. Yes, this is a simplification, since it seems easier to rely on a machine, and yet it is a misguided simplification.

Why? There are many reasons. Technology has a narrowly

defined function and performs only that. Any change in functionality requires upgrading, changes, or new equipment altogether. With changing threats, equipment can quickly become irrelevant or obsolete but remain un-replaced because of budgetary constraints.

When using technology, there is a latent assumption that it fully replaces people. But technology needs people to install, calibrate, operate, and maintain it; thus, its real performance still depends on people. Moreover, this delegation of responsibility relaxes agents' intellect and alertness. Their focus is now on operating technology instead of on detecting threats. A common example is that of a metal detector whose sensitivity is set by an operator. Set the sensitivity too high, and the machine sets off too many alarms at every piece of metal, resulting in alarms being ignored, including ones that have detected a real threat (just like house alarms are often ignored). Set the sensitivity too low, and the machine will not set off an alarm when necessary. Both cases can result in actual security threats being missed.

Reread the case described in the Introduction on how long lines led to the use of a magnetometer alongside an X-ray full-body scanner, with both machines having different detection capabilities.

Technology does drop responsibility back into our human laps; it does so differently during power failures, equipment malfunction, hacker attacks, or other service-breaking events. Thus, the psychological riddance of responsibility is incorrect because while we think our bases are covered, most are exposed.

In security, we must consider such potential failures, breaches, and attacks on equipment, communications and computers, the criminal exploitation of performance and technological weak points, and breaches in the way equipment is used. We do this to develop countermeasures, firewalls, specific security measures, and procedures whose nature is to respond mostly to experience. Why do we respond to experience? Because that is what we normally do. In a previous chapter, we discussed how basing responses on experience makes them predictable and easier for fast-moving, sneaky perpetrators to stay a step ahead of us. Technology is equally affected by this mindset in which perpetrators identify equipment shortcomings, maliciously exploiting them.

An additional aspect is that of technology being unable to perform as well as properly trained humans. A good example of this is SBInet, or the Secure Border Initiative Network, a 2006 initiative from the US Department of Homeland Security. The idea was to have a virtual fence along the US-Mexico border that would use various technologies, such as thermal-recognition systems, video and other identification technologies, to secure that border. But after over a billion dollars had been spent, the project was stopped. Why? For several reasons: (i) Technologies cannot stop perpetrators from crossing the border, they only identify them; (ii) weather, topography, flora and fauna affect detection conditions like line of sight, level of false alarms or failed detection, in short – the quality of pre-emptive information; (iii) actual prevention is done by ground forces, not by equipment. Adapting the technology to above stated differing and ever changing environmental conditions was found to be more difficult than anticipated and the technology less adaptable to different geographical areas than thought. The bottom line was that the technology used for SBInet was incapable of replicating the performance of technology-assisted humans. It could not "see" or "hear" in the human sense of those words, nor could it smell distinctive odors, detect tracks, or put together seemingly disparate pieces of information to form an educated guess about a possible outcome in a situation it hadn't faced before. It could not substitute for a well-trained border agent.

This situation also exists in the US-Canadian border, which receives less attention than the southern US border. An article in the *New York Times International Edition* describes the situation:[22]

> Cameras along the border recently showed [in one instance] four men dressed in camouflage outfits who appeared to have weapons crossing the border. Agents never caught them. Another camera image showed a group of about half a dozen people walking through the woods at night across the border. Agents said they had no infor-

---

[22] https://www.nytimes.com/2016/10/17/us/northern-border-illicit-crossing.html?_r=0

mation on the group.

"These guys make me nervous," Mr. Curtis [acting division chief for the Border Patrol Swanton Division] said. "My technology can show me when someone makes an entry, but it can't tell me who they are, and we can't always get there in time to catch them."

Our conclusion is that reliance on technology alone is a simplification error, since the ultimate responsibility lies with us anyway. Delegating human responsibility to machines is not enough to guarantee an effective outcome, especially when the technology itself depends on humans.

The Strategic and Macro Perspective

We also need to look at technology from the perspective of how it is utilized as part of a security-system strategy.

Technology and People

The first driver is a mistaken assumption that technology in general has the power to compensate for human gaps in ability and performance. Yes, it compensates for very specific abilities under specified conditions. Yet, this argument is debatable because of the equipment's dependence on humans to operate it and to design, manufacture, install, calibrate, and maintain the equipment. Lapses in any of the human interventions in creating and operating a machine will naturally reduce its reliability in terms of the security role the machine fulfills.

Today's true role of technology is to enhance human sensory, process and memory abilities. CCTVs replace eyesight, microphones improve hearing, metal detectors replace our hands, face recognition replaces our eyesight and brain. They do it consistently, faster, and with better memory. But, as previously discussed, they are limited requiring constant human intervention raising the question; is technology assisted by humans or, humans assisted by technology? The later is the winning formula while the former reduces the human into part of the machine. Understanding the limits of technology and of specific equipment is therefore essential. For example, full-body X-ray scanners do not detect rigid objects side-carried by people.[23] Making proper use of such scanners requires that each person be scanned twice, a prohibitive practice for airports and crowded areas. If we scan once we may miss concealed weapons, but if the human factor focuses on the public, not on the machine, it may identify suspicious behavior and call the person aside for a manual check. This would occur only if the human is assisted by technology, not vice versa and, it will probably be much more effective than computer-selected random checks.

Technology also deflects security attention away from real

---

[23] https://www.radsec.org/secure1000-sec14.pdf;
https://professional-troublemaker.com/2012/03/06/1b-of-nude-body-scanners-made-worthless-by-blog-how-anyone-can-get-anything-past-the-tsas-nude-body-scanners/; "An evaluation of airport x-ray backscatter units based on image characteristics," Leon Kaufman, Joseph W. Carlson, Journal of Transportation Security, March 2011, Volume 4, Issue 1, pp 73–94.

security to dealing with whatever is detected, like drugs or confiscating totally harmless *Star Wars* lightsaber swords. Yes, agents choose or are instructed to react to these, but this is precisely where actions strongly diverge from the mission and vision. Machines provide information, and people react on it, but does the machine provide threat-related information? Do operators understand that drugs and *Star Wars* saber swords have nothing to do with security?

Operators react on machine alarms, which are partly not trustworthy because of the objects detected, equipment's false-alarm[24] and nuisance-alarm rates.[25] The question arises: If we need staff, and the equipment does not provide false-free threat detection, should it have been procured to begin with?

I was invited to assess the security of a seaside nuclear power station in a certain country. Perimeter intrusion detection included three parallel systems that theoretically backed each other up. After a discussion with management, I started interviewing the field personnel, those who have the best touch and feel of the system.

One of my questions was "How many false alarms do you have?"

The gentleman said, "Thirty."

I asked, "Thirty a month?"

"No, thirty a day," he said.

---

[24] False alarms caused by the inherent physics and design of a machine, like radars detecting background objects.

[25] False alarms caused, for example, by vegetation growth in front of an IR detector.

"So, your detection system is practically non-existent?" I asked.

"Yes," was his answer, "we rely only on staff."

The systems chosen were technologically and otherwise unfit to work in the foggy, humid, marine environment of the power station. Is this a singular case? No.

Procurement and Performance

Equipment procurement policies are made at very high levels, all the way up to the secretary of the DHS. Acquisition entails huge budgets, either because of the quantity of equipment required (metal detectors, for example) or because of the performance of equipment required. As we discussed in the section about capital expenditure, large budgets become traps–an ego and performance trap–for two reasons.

Firstly, people like to feel powerful, and some of that thirst for power can be quenched by pushing ahead large expenditures. "I manage a $1-billion budget" is an impressive statement, though once one understands what is behind that statement and what such an expenditure actually achieves, that impression may drastically change. It is not so impressive if the speaker manages a $1-billion budget share out of a total $1-trillion budget, for example. Nor is it quite so astounding if the speaker has spent that money on the wrong concept, or the wrong supplier, as with SBInet. And as already stated, it is, however, far "sexier" to have spent $1 billion on equipment and technology than it is to have spent it on payrolls and training, even when efficient, able, and good agents would be the result of more payroll spending.

Secondly, the actual choice of equipment does define certain limitations of the system we call HLS, impacting the fulfillment of the detection-and-prevention role. It may seem obvious, but by choosing one technology over another, one machine over a different one with maybe different performance, the entire system gains not only a possible new set of abilities (say, "face and mood recognition") but also a new set of limitations like expensive, budget-consuming equipment, giving up the use of personnel, or face-recognition limitations. But when big money is involved, industry competition and pressures are huge, sometimes pushing to procure from better-connected suppliers and possibly away from a better-performing, but unconnected company. And once equipment is purchased, the entire organization then experiences the implications of the choice made. With this in mind, looking again to the TSA's failed detection test, this is no coincidence, since the same procedures and technology choice was applied to most or all locations, which now suffer from the same constraints of that choice.

But equipment also has another facet of inflexibility. Most security-related detection systems are closed systems with well-defined specifications and performance. The systems are based on physical principles, which themselves have their limitations and boundaries; thus, once a design is made, it is fixed with minor performance flexibility if at all. Lack of flexibility implies that equipment cannot evolve as threats do, leading to frequent and costly equipment replacement or upgrade. No one will re-invest in equipment upgrade or new equipment every time the performance of older machines fails to detect a new type of threat. The result is that outdated equipment is expected to detect threats that it cannot possibly identify.

When equipment is evaluated for purchasing, it should be clear what it does, but it should also be clear what it doesn't do and what has to be complemented to achieve the required HLS system performance. The system's useful threat-detection lifespan must also be assessed by imagining what new, creative solutions perpetrators may come up with to circumvent equipment detection like the current threat of packing explosives into working lap tops.[26]

An example of how poorly technology can be handled is that of HLS radio failure.[27] During 9/11, poor communication between agents and agencies was blamed on radios, with radios failing to be compatible with each other or frequencies being different, or even some agencies not allowing others to use their frequencies. Technically, this problem should be fairly easy to solve, and in fact almost $430 million have been thrown at the problem over the last fifteen years. And yet a report from the Homeland Security Office of Inspector Gen-

---

[26] http://edition.cnn.com/2017/03/21/politics/electronics-ban-devices-explosives-intelligence/

[27] http://www.npr.org/sections/thetwo-way/2015/06/08/412919097/after-spending-millions-on-communications-homeland-security-fails-radio-test

eral in 2012 found that less than 0.25% of DHS radios tested could access the channel that had been earmarked as the common communication frequency. In this case, the technology is one that could fairly be assumed to be safe to rely on–after all, a radio makes no decisions; its only job is to allow agents to communicate. And yet even here we see human failures that could be catastrophic under the right circumstances.

To summarize, technology has a role in HLS when well-planned, used, maintained, and well-understood. Technology takes some of the onus of overworked agents, leaving them free to concentrate on matters that can't be handled through or by technology. Technology is absolutely no substitute for well-trained HLS personnel and, despite constant technological evolution, is unlikely to ever be a substitute for the human factor. It can only complement it.

Now we come to an essential question: Can HLS work?

Can Homeland Security Work?

By failing to prepare, you are preparing to fail.
— Benjamin Franklin

Allow me to skip to the end and say that yes, Homeland Security can work, and in fact mostly does work. However, the real question is: Will Homeland Security continue to work in the face of increasing world turmoil? In the face of wars, jihad, exoduses, refugees, cyber and other crime, and an increasing cultural mix under the auspices of the liberal West? This is a far more challenging question.

HLS: A Perspective

There was a time when traveling and communications were both time consuming and costly, and that time was not all that long ago. As an example, from the beginning of the 1950s until 2013, the number of airline passengers has increased steadily from practically zero to some seven billion passengers per year. Globalization has led to the same with cargo, with trade, with movement of know-how, knowledge, money, and commodities. These can all be good things, but the price that we pay for this is that refuge seekers, terrorists, and criminals exploit the ease, comfort, and accessibility of our developed world, as well as its opportunities, and knowhow.

The challenge faced by HLS is therefore increasing exponentially in terms of both quantity and quality, resulting from accessibility to technologies, ease of transportation, access to information and Do-It-Yourself solutions. Go online and you find detailed instructions on how to make a bomb; go a step further and enter the Darknet, and you can buy a bomb, drugs, art, 3D files to print guns and more. What in the past required a widespread support network can now be discreetly executed with a few people, a bank transfer or anonymous bitcoin, some money laundering, and some easily available information. One example is the San Bernardino killers, who took a legal loan and then bought arms from American dealers to exercise their malice.

The simplicity of planning a terrorist attack and the accessibility to information combined with Western naivety and a "live-and-let-live" attitude are great drivers of freedom, knowledge, and economic growth, but are also the biggest challenge faced by HLS. When looking at certain countries and cultures, one finds that some are closed to Western values; no church would be allowed, no sharing of the principles of Western life. So clearly the people flux is out of such closed countries, moving from the hard to the soft, heading toward Western acceptance and openness.

This generates a contradiction because, as previously touched upon, immigrants want to live in the West because the way of life is enabling and positive, and success is a result of hard work, intelligence, and skills rather than because of family background, for example. However, though many seek a new life in the West, some exploit the Western leniency toward crime or seek to destroy the West through terror, drugs, crime, or enslavement. Thus, the enemy security forces are up against is within, as seen in the 2016 Orlando shootings; in France, where 84 people were murdered in Nice on Bastille Day by an immigrant; and in Wurzburg, Germany, where an Afghan immigrant murdered one and wounded several others with an axe.

Add to this the already-discussed fact that perpetrators are like water–block them here and they simply find a new route, thus creating vast opportunities to materialize security threats, seemingly stacking the odds against HLS. This is the case with drug trafficking, for example, where, despite the impressive quantities of contraband seized each year, suppliers are still able to satisfy most of the market demand, keeping prices as high as they want.

The more we invest in trench warfare, simply defending our own territory, the lower the probability is of succeeding and winning this war on public safety and the Western way of life. The battlefield should be moved to the perpetrator's back yard, into their networks, families, and support circles. It is through people, intelligence, maneuver warfare or "battle in motion", and being more creative than the perpetrators themselves that the battles, one by one, will be won.

And yes, to some extent this is already happening, but the question is whether the ratio of proactive countermeasures and passive defensive methods should not be skewed more toward proactive HLS activities.

HLS: In Practice

Western laws and constitutions are very much focused on the human rights of the individual, thereby imposing a great, and mostly justified, burden on those officers of the law who are dedicated to protecting our values and to ensuring (as far as possible) justice and fair treatment to all. To ensure that laws are followed, rules and procedures are created, which further limit the judgment of individual officers in specific situations. This is not to say that failures don't occur due to personality, wrong decisions, lack of judgment, or fear–they do. The point is that we strive to cross all the t's, dot all the i's, check off all the checklists, and yet HLS still doesn't always work. The reasons for this have been covered already: lack of soul and attentiveness, focus on detection instead of on procedures, and the fact that when trusted most people try harder than when simply bound by procedure; thereby, trust increases the "sensory" radius of HLS. But billions of US dollars and almost 500,000 additional employees later, can current Homeland Security strategy work?

To answer that question, let us turn to the *Washington Post*, which in 2010 published a lengthy series of articles by Dana Priest and William M. Arkin. For over two years, Priest and Arkin investigated what they refer to as "Top Secret America"–discussing the systems put in place to ensure US safety, including HLS.[28] Their project was based on public records and interviews with government and security officials. What was found was that the infrastructure created to protect America from terrorism has become so massive that its "effectiveness is impossible to determine." To understand just how unwieldy that HLS agency has become, look at the following figures cited by Priest and Arkin:

- Over 3,000 companies, both governmental and private, are involved in work related to HLS in some form, spread out over 10,000 US locations;

- Over 850,000 people hold top-secret security clearance;

- Overlap between agencies doing the same work creates redundancy, where, for example, 51 separate organizations are devoted to tracking terrorist money around the country;

- Approximately 50,000 intelligence reports are published each year, resulting in a paper trail so long that many reports are simply ignored.

From these and other findings, it's easy to see that in practice HLS organizations are far from efficient and, inefficiency

---

[28] http://projects.washingtonpost.com/top-secret-america/articles/a-hidden-world-growing-beyond-control/

leads to ineffectiveness. With so much overlap and so many people, properties, and paperwork to oversee, it is 'hard to see the forest for the trees'. But the *Washington Post* project does not stand alone. In 2009, Army Lieutenant General John R. Vines was tasked with reviewing how the Department of Defense tracked its sensitive programs. In his own words: "I'm not aware of any agency with the authority, responsibility or a process in place to coordinate all these interagency and commercial activities. The complexity of this system defies description."

The bottom line is that because the system in practice is so huge and so, dare I say it, lacking coordination, its efficacy simply can't be determined. As Vines puts it: "Because it lacks a synchronizing process, it inevitably results in message dissonance, reduced effectiveness and waste. We consequently can't effectively assess whether it is making us safer."

Our question was can *current* HLS strategy work, and the answer we've come up with is maybe unsatisfactory, that we frankly just don't know if it can work because the system in place is so large and cumbersome that we cannot effectively evaluate it. While saying that we cannot judge something is not the same as saying that something does not work, it seems fair to draw the conclusion that the situation could be improved, if only to make things more organized so that the system could be evaluated, each goal or target by itself as well as the interface between them.

So much for theory; let us look at more concrete examples

of why or why not the current HLS system may not be as prepared to meet future threats as we'd like.

Fighting the Last War: TSA as an Example

Let us begin with one simple and, for some people, surprising fact: the TSA has never caught a terrorist. Why? They were focused on addressing security flaws that had already been taken advantage of, rather than preventing future security flaws and closing (still) existing back doors. Will the TSA, as an example, ever apprehend a terrorist? Probably not, for several reasons:

- Travel and air terror are particularly well prepared. This is not a passing-by burglar identifying a seemingly empty house, breaking in and running off if the alarm sounds. This means that aviation perpetrators are especially difficult to identify and apprehend;

- Attacking air travelers can also take place on the ground, just like the 2016 attack in Brussels International Airport, which was coordinated with another suicide bomber in a metro station;

- See the previously discussed issue of the massive and rigid security organization vs. the entrepreneurial, well-funded terrorist;

- Should a perpetrator reach an aircraft, whether he succeeds or not in creating damage, points at a major intelligence flaw, leaving the TSA as the last line of defense.

149

And yet even a well-prepared perpetrator leaves finger-prints, and if these fingerprints are not detected using intelligence, such as in 9/11, then the chances that TSA gate or employee checks, or pre-screened passenger lists will detect perpetrators are extremely low;

- The already-discussed ease of communications and travel, smaller support rings, and the vast number of op-portunities for malicious activities, like sending damag-ing cargo or using Shoulder-fired missiles, all mean that pre-detection is extremely difficult, and close to impos-sible.

All of this becomes especially true when considering passport forgery operations by organizations such as the Islamic State, and activities including smuggling of terrorists into the West under the guise of refugees.

The TSA is in no position to guarantee that they can pre-vent terrorists from disrupting air travel. But what about other potential security breaches?

The Protection of Critical Installations

As mentioned many times, there is no end to the imagination of determined perpetrators, and to illustrate that point, and the point that protecting critical installations is more difficult than you may imagine, let us look at a Latin American oil com-pany whose oil (crude and other) is subject to frequent stealing.

150

Here is just one "thread" in the company's battle against such stealing:

- **Malicious Action**: The stealing began with falsified shipping papers and loading trucks painted to look like oil company trucks;

- **Response**: In reaction to this, the company equipped their trucks with tracking and other devices for logistics people to verify trucks' true location and identity;

- **Malicious Action**: The perpetrators then moved on to simply hijacking company trucks instead;

- **Response**: The company added more security, with some success;

- **Malicious Action**: The perpetrators then moved on to raiding installations, stealing oil-loaded company trucks from inside the installations.

Malicious activities continued outside the critical installations including threatening drivers and their families leading to oil transfer from company tankers to perpetrator tankers. Perpetrators disguise themselves as police units, setting up road blocks and hijacking tankers.

The story goes on, but the methodology is clear. There is always another crack in the rock, always another way forward. The company thinks of blocking an opening, fixing a flaw, but, not being a security company, it fails to think of what the next twist could be. This illustrates perfectly the potential flaws in the defensive systems of protecting critical installations, what-ever those installations may be.

Protecting Crowds

Crowd protection is the most complex challenge–crowds are in the streets, theaters, stadiums, demonstrations, street marches, marathons, and more. Crowds are convenient, high-profile tar-gets easily creating the impact terrorists seek.

We have seen the impact of such attacks in the 2013 Boston Marathon, with 3 dead and over 260 wounded; the Bataclan theater attack in Paris, with 129 dead and 352 wounded; and the 2016 Bastille Day attack in Nice, which resulted in 85 dead and 434 wounded.

Crowd protection is about public awareness and police screening and fencing (virtual or real). Isolate the specific crowd from the public and screen those entering the venue or area, even when a parade advances along a street. Screening is about faces, behaviors, winter coats on summer days, or heavy and overstuffed backpacks. It is about cunning and should be met with cunning, awareness and knowledge, imagination, sus-picion, and people profiling. Technology has a limited contri-bution in crowded, especially open, venues. It is the public, security agents, and uniformed police whose alertness, sharp eyes, and gut feelings are the key to early perpetrator identifi-cation and prevention.

Here again, there is no one-size-fits-all solution for pro-tecting such events. Security chiefs need to tailor their security concept to each event, using respective means, awareness, imagination and alertness to meet the list of potential threats and beyond.

Closing the Cycle

We can also look at defensive protection in the light of seemingly good decisions that have been ill thought out. As an example, consider a steel mill in South America that employs 20,000 people and suffers from the theft of copper and aluminum electrical cables, which have electrocuted many thieves. This includes a 100-kilovolt underground cable that, apart from being very expensive, fed into most of the mill's internal plants. So, when it was stolen, the plants simply shut down, including furnaces that take a week to reheat.

Company engineers proposed the installation of sensors with alarms on all high-voltage cable access points. What the engineers failed to consider, though, was what would be the reaction should the alarms sound. What was to be done upon unauthorized opening of an underground cable access point? Sending a hired, low-cost security guard was not an option, since all perpetrators would have to do is to threaten him ("You want to see your family tonight? Then go!"). Similarly, police forces, or rather the policemen themselves, wished to return home safely and would turn a blind eye to matters–a cultural issue.

Rather than complicating the detect-react loop, maybe a better way of dealing with the theft issue would have been to simply prevent access to the cable in the first place. The creation of a higher barrier of entry, for example, so that only well-prepared, heavily equipped and determined robbers could succeed in stealing the cable. Such theft cannot be stopped completely, but its frequency can be reduced. There will always be an alternative method—maybe a more complex one, but it does exist. The point is that even when we think we're doing the right thing, we're not always doing so, through lack of communication, lack of understanding, or other biases.

The Key: People

So far the news has been all bad, and you would be right in protesting that at the beginning of this chapter I stated that Homeland Security can work. All I have done is tell you why its work is flawed. And yet, yes, HLS can work, and the key to its success is people, their creativity, imagination, paranoia, awareness, alertness, and senses, all of which increase detection-and-prevention probability and success. People working proactively, creating that previously discussed Maneuver Warfare or battle in motion that will move the fight into the perpetrators' back yard. This is done in drug enforcement and in terror prevention as well, but maybe it should also be applied to HLS in its strictest sense, reducing the static and noticeable trench lines in return for more intellectual freedom for staff.

Care must be taken not to flip the coin altogether and become too intrusive or totalitarian, like with Communist-era KGB informant methods, which were so effective that fear alone was enough to dissuade many "revolutionaries." Our freedom-led innovation, philosophy, and growth can and should lead the war on malice because there doesn't seem to be any other culture willing to do so.

Let us turn, then, to how we can make this work, how people can improve the efficiency of HLS and improve its outcomes.

Developing Defensive Security

First we form habits, then they form us.

So, after all we have discussed so far, how does one go about designing a security system that actually works? I have placed a heavy emphasis on the importance of people, and I stand by this; but people, of course, cannot work in a vacuum. Yes, procedures, rules, and equipment as well as organization are all necessary for well-trained agents to do their jobs effectively. Our goal is to have the 'system' support agents in delivering security and not have agents serve the system and its bureaucracy. The following describes the typical stages of developing defensive security, but we must always keep in mind that it is the personnel who are going to be the key players here. The system must be built around people and serve them in doing their job rather than have them adhere to the system.

This chapter provides general guidelines and points to reflect on; it is not intended to be a universal checklist for security designs.

Defensive Security Solutions

As discussed, defensive security solutions are stationary or dynamic elements, mostly comprising security personnel and equipment whose roles are dissuasion, prevention, and reaction in the face of emergency or event management. As discussed, the key challenge is that security organizations, especially their staff, must be alert for the unexpected, anytime, anyplace.

It would be unfair to expect agents, as well trained as they may be, to act purely alone. And for this reason, it is necessary to develop security organizations, systems *they*, the agents, can rely on and can work within while still retaining their flexibility and a certain amount of freedom. This is the opposite of abiding to, and serving the 'system'. And no, procedures should not be deliberately and consistently disobeyed, but neither should they be blindly obeyed if a positive outcome obviously depends on disobeying them. In fact, procedures and structures should be designed, wherever possible, as guidelines to try and avoid this conundrum in the first place. Good defensive security systems inherently support this key human element.

Stages of Defensive Security Development

There are six key stages in designing effective security solutions, whether for corporate security, HLS, or any other form of security solution. The breadth and depth of each stage depends on the scope of the security task defined by the "owner" of the protected asset including its type, size, mobility, importance, and value.[29] The decisions made during the conceptualization and design phases of each stage strongly impact solution effectivity, personnel, equipment, flexibility and costs. Biases, errors, and overestimation can critically hamper security results.

Developing security solutions along the below-stated lines combined with people-centric thinking, awareness to biases, and thinking of medium-term risk dynamics helps achieve better and sustainable security.

Let's look at each in detail:

1. Risk Analysis and Threat Assessment

Before developing a defensive security solution, it's essential that first we know our goal: what are we protecting and what are we protecting against? Therefore, the first stage in this process is always risk assessment and subsequent threat assessment for the specific assets(s), which consists of the following steps:

- Study the asset: locations, routines, weak points, mobility, and access routes. Assets can be people, trucks moving valuables, information, buildings, compounds, ships, or aircraft. Each has its own profile;

- Area-wide information gathering: this may involve intelligence gathering on known or perceived threats,

---

[29] Value can be monetary, knowhow, public profile, etc.

location-specific and wide-area risks, related structures or elements that may affect protection, past events, or special requirements such as used when moving an important personage from one place to another;

- Criticality assessment (asset-centric) is the stage in which it is decided what and/or whom needs to be protected, when, and where. The result is an asset list ordered by importance (like value, high profile, high importance, secrecy) and setting the priority of asset protection under a variety of contexts like locations, situations, or events. The priority list defines focus in routine and emergency;

- Threat assessment (threat-centric): the identification and analysis of threats on assets based on information from step one as well as known, estimated, or perceived capability and motivation of possible perpetrators. This should be done remembering that perpetrators are creative, agile, and like water!

- Vulnerability and consequence assessments: requires a wide analysis of a variety of issues like what would be the consequence of a realistic criminal or terror scenario when attacking your defined targets? What is at risk? Would that outcome differ if, for example, different kinds of explosives, weapons, falsification, posing or other methods were used? Other asset-attack-result scenarios should be analyzed without limiting the creativity of the team. Unrealistic scenarios should always be considered;

- Scenario prioritization: is the result of integrating the asset-centric analysis, threat-centric analysis, and the vulnerability/consequence assessment in which the realistic asset-scenarios are prioritized. The parameters according to which priorities are set vary and should be defined by the designer. These include risk, image, value, public impact, loss of lives, damaged buildings, transportation disruption, or other forms of "cost." The result is also what will not be protected under certain circumstances, like in chess when a piece is sacrificed. This stage sets the basis for the conceptual and later detailed designs.

The goal of this first stage is information gathering and analysis. Once this stage is completed, the goals of and expectations from the future system will be clear, leading to a focused and effective solution to handle security threats. Given that the human factor is put in the forefront and listened to, an effective organization will be in place, as opposed to an unwieldy, procedure- and machine-driven HLS organization.

In addition, much like a business plan, the security plan should be reviewed periodically (like once a year), upon receiving intelligence, learning from the experience of others, and after significant events. Security is a live and dynamic matter requiring professionalism, constant adaptation, and perseverance.

2. Strategy Formulation

Once stage one has been completed, it is then necessary to put together a high-level vision of the defense solution that will be designed. This is the big picture, the goal to be kept in mind when designing and operating the system, the "elevator pitch." The vision is then converted into a strategy, a Mitigation Strategy, a plan of action designed to meet a major goal–in our case, defensive security. The strategy can make use of land, sea, and air elements; it may be static or dynamic; it details how and how early should people and elements detect and prevent malicious acts.

It is important to remember that converting a vision to strategy and then to implementation involves human biases as well as simplification dictated by technical or other details. Bias awareness helps avoid putting form over essence, prioritizing technical issues over system requirements, and preferring procedures over people.

This big picture determines all else, is the spirit communicated to staff and agents; it is their end goal, their north star for navigation and for making extra-procedural decisions.

3. High-level Implementation Concept

This is the high-level design that turns the strategy into practical realities like block diagrams or flow charts that translate the strategy into high-level executables, specific goals, staffing, means, and scope of work. Such concepts have many facets and lots of designer flexibility because flow, equipment, and personnel can be combined in many ways and still achieve the same goal and performance. It is at this stage and the next one that the trap of capital investments becomes evident.

Assuming the same level of security is achieved, what differs between solutions is their cost (operating and capital), flexibility when different reactions are required, adaptability to meet changing threats, and additional cost of such adaptation. Thus, a key challenge is to look ahead and bring to life concepts that can be adapted to that future required, (normally) threat-driven, change. Concepts should not be limited to the here and now, making them costly down the line; they should include forward thinking.

The high-level concept also touches on how vulnerabilities are addressed, dissuasion and prevention means, personnel, methods of communication, command & control concepts and elements, and procedures.

4. Detailed Design

When the core concept, block diagram, or architecture is in place, it is broken down into four key elements:

- **People**: including guard or agent profiles, training requirements, managers and management strategy, command & control operators, and their qualifications. A training curriculum and methodology will also be set up

163

to ensure that personnel are not only initially suitable for their roles but that they *continue* to be so;

- **Equipment**: including specifications, communications and networking requirements, interfaces, calibration instructions, and equipment necessary for running a control center. Normally, construction and infrastructure requirements like an expanded communications network, escape routes, electric cabling, and more roadways are included;

- **Procedures**: both routine and emergency reactions, actions, and behaviors. These should not be restrictive to the point of dissuading staff from using personal judgment, experience, and pure common sense in any given situation. Procedures should be detailed enough that a security agent will not lack support or training when faced with a truly unexpected event but, should be short and concise for agents to remember. Cooperation with police, the Red Cross, and other agencies may also be included here–who works alongside whom, and who provides information, assistance, communication channels and so on;

- **Intelligence**: how third-party and local intelligence will be gathered, centralized, and reported; how it will be used to assess new threats or re-assess old ones; how it will affect current procedures and priorities; and how operational intelligence is relayed to agents in the field.

At this stage, a check is required looking for human bias, dilution, and simplification of the vision. As discussed, the need to convert the general vision into specifics entails omissions, simplifications, real-life constraints, and other such factors that more than once either deviate the plan from the vision or reduce the vision to a simplistic and limited solution.

Thus, the design of all elements must be firmly focused on the human factor from those that develop the concepts all the way to those operating the system. We need to encourage project leaders and staff to be aware, communicate, give feedback; we need to allow flexibility rather than restrictions, and support them rather than impose on them.

The detailed design also serves as the basis for project costing and bidding.

5. *Installation and Integration*

With the detailed design in hand and suppliers selected, we move on to the implementation stage, the logistics of putting said designs into place. This includes installation of equipment, any construction that may be necessary, hiring and training of qualified personnel, writing procedures, and establishing communication channels–both personal and technical infrastructure. Then the system is put to work, tested to the full extent of the vision and strategy it is designed to meet. This includes putting agents, operators, and equipment through operational tests and stress.

While it may not be possible to define one certain type of

security agent that is being looked for, there are certain characteristics that are to be sought. Quick thinking, initiative taking, persistence, and perception are highly valued. Creativity, bravery, and flexibility are also important. Without going into the politics of governmental or private company economics, we already discussed the general truth that within limits, the better paid someone is, the better he or she will tend to perform at a job, so payroll budget must also be accounted for. Security is a profession in which well-paid, well-trained agents are an asset to any organization.

6. *The Follow-up*
Once the security system is in place, there are several important follow-up steps:

- **Plan, review, and update**: must be done to ensure the system and its organization are adapted to meet current and potential future threats;

- **Operation**: routine operation must be continually evaluated for efficacy. Any flaws must be identified and solved, and failures studied to ensure they aren't repeated;

- **Training**: personnel must be kept trained up to standard. The emergence of new threats requires new awareness and countermeasures. Training may be specific to a certain position or location, but there should also be full-scale training in which all guards, managers, out-

166

side agencies, and field agents participate to share experiences and learn from each other;

- **Exercises and simulations**: are run on a regular basis to ensure that personnel retain alertness and that training is up to standard;

- **Audits**: periodical system, personnel, and equipment audits are done. Audits of the systems' individual components are also done to ensure the organization, department, and personnel are fulfilling their missions within the periodically adjusted and re-evaluated list of threats, of assets, and malicious scenarios.

To summarize, security designs are by people, for people, and thus must bear in mind people–from design and operation to security and serving the public. Secondly, being conceived by people, awareness to our biases will improve their end performance.

Conclusions

And so, we come to an end. The threats that nations, agents, and people such as you and I face are very real. The perpetrators are motivated, cunning, fast moving, exploit Western openness, and work with small support circles and fast decision making. But the picture I wish to paint is not one of failure or one of lost hope. HLS exists for a reason, and there are many factors that are clearly working. And yet there are others that are not. Our goal should be to strive for improvement, to seek to protect ourselves as best we are able. And that means making changes. What are our take-home lessons here?

Back to the Beginning

Allow me to return to the very beginning of this book, the introduction. Queuing in the airport, having witnessed the flaws in the HLS system first-hand, was I in danger? Probably not, but possibly so. As an end consumer of the HLS product (albeit one perhaps more security educated than the normal end user), I expect a certain experience, a service, and that service is the security and safety of me and those around me.

We have discussed many elements of the HLS puzzle, from intelligence to technology, interagency cooperation to decision making, leadership to simplification sins. And in the previous chapter, developing defensive solutions have been covered. If HLS is to rise to the challenge of a changing world, if it is to protect us and our own from small, fast-acting cells, then certain changes must be made. I hope in the course of this book, those changes have been thoroughly covered. But there is one major factor that deserves to be revisited. If you remember nothing else from this book, remember this: that HLS will succeed or fail based on the human factor.

The Human Factor

That all-important human factor is so essential in any security system—or any organization, for that matter. While the approaches outlined in this book can help create effective security solutions, these can only be as good as the people strategizing, developing, and operating them. Agents must be given the guidelines and tools they need to react and execute a successful detection, prevention, and disaster-management plan. Agents restricted by hard and fast rules will be prevented from being effective. Therefore, expectations both of personnel themselves and the system that is being designed around them should be made clear. It is the sanity check of implementation against our north star, our vision and strategy:

Each security agent–whether an X-ray technician, security guard, or agent in any other role–maintains a certain responsibility. This means that agents are expected to think; keep their eyes open; identify behaviors, flaws, and uncalibrated equipment; and act–not simply operate machines or "work by the book."

Personnel should be allowed to profile people, detect threats, prevent disruption, and delay suspected perpetrators; and agents should not be enslaved either to the means of doing so (whether technology or procedures) or to their superiors. Yes, both management and procedures are necessary in a smoothly run organization, but these must be flexible, trusting, and courageous enough to delegate, to allow for creative thinking and outside-the-box actions, and in consequence to fulfill the vision for which the security is in place to begin with. And yes, rules are to be broken if necessary;

Good, well-trained personnel and agents are essential, and (stating the obvious) that means hiring agents with the right personality, daring, and intellect; paying a decent salary; and keeping personnel motivated, as well as allowing for flexibility when it comes to procedures and outcomes. There are certain times when the end does indeed justify the means, and if a successful outcome is achieved, it may not matter whether protocol was directly followed; nor will "following procedures" and failing help. At the end of the day, our life heroes are not the conformists, but those who thought out of the box, who dared to break the rules and succeeded.

The Future of HLS

As we discussed in the introduction, HLS has a mission to fulfill. Arguably, it is currently fulfilling this mission, though we could also argue that it is not doing it effectively or in the right fashion. What is very clear, however, is that the world is rapidly changing, and to continue to fulfill the mission appointed to it, HLS must also change.

The mission of detecting and preventing criminal and terrorist acts is no simple matter, but there are lessons to be learned from past mistakes, from previous experience, and even from the business world. If HLS is to continue to protect us, our families, and our homelands, then these lessons must be considered: Trust people to become faster and more intelligent. Trust people and reduce outdated bureaucracy which will also reduce overall cost of homeland security organizations and free up budgets for better people.

Make no mistake: the next crisis, the next act of terrorism, the next tragedy, is certain to happen. It is probably already being planned. It is essential, if our world and the values we love are to be protected, that HLS can rise to the challenge of defeating this act, whatever it may be. And it is only by honest evaluation and criticism of mistakes, honest decision making, honest estimation of strengths and weaknesses, and (most of all) through the employment of honest, aware, motivated people with clear yet flexible goals, that this can be achieved.

About the Author

Mr. Jephtah Lorch has decades of experience holding C-level executive positions in industry, leading major Homeland Security projects and conducting business worldwide. He is involved in security and Homeland Security since 1994.

Nowadays Mr. Lorch is applying his extensive CEO experience focusing on strategy consulting and executive mentoring in security and industry.

Mr. Lorch led security projects of up to $400M from risk assessment and concept development through project management and delivery. Projects include oil & gas, utilities, telecoms, industry, borders, safe cities, consulting to decision makers and more.

As CEO Mr. Lorch turned around a bankrupt wireless equipment company sold to a NASDAQ-traded corporation, merged a telecom equipment company into a NYSE-traded conglomerate, made an exit from an optical company and managed several other technology companies.

Mr. Lorch's first book: Business is Decisions, Success is Intuition mirrors his people-oriented approach, extensive international and cross-cultural experience, and interest in historical processes.

Made in the USA
Coppell, TX
19 October 2019

10287284R10105